Robert
Pattinson
Eternally Yours

To Colleen AF Venable, who inspires

The author would like to thank Martha Mihalick and
Molly O'Neill for their invaluable contributions to this project.

Insert: pages 1, 2, 3 (top), 5, 8, © The Barnes Theatre Company; pages 3 (middle),
4 (top), © JIL Studio/Getty Images; page 4 (bottom), © Fred Duval/Getty Images;
pages 3 (bottom), 6, 7, © Amy Howe Photography.

Library of Congress Cataloging-in-Publication Data is available.
ISBN 978-0-06-176553-7

Typography by Pamela Darcy of Neo9 Design, Inc.

First Edition

Robert Pattinson

Eternally Yours

An Unauthorized Biography

By Isabelle Adams

HarperEntertainment
An Imprint of HarperCollins*Publishers*

Contents

Introduction

Be Still Our Hearts!

Robert Pattinson never expected to be haunting the dreams of millions of teenage girls around the world. In fact, the thousands of screaming fans usually make him blush! But this gifted (and stunningly attractive) young actor better get used to the attention because his starring role as the world's hottest vampire has secured his spot in our hearts.

In just two breakout roles, Robert Pattinson has gone from being a minor hottie to an all-out, major heartthrob. And he's gone from extreme to extreme as far as the roles he's played. In the movie adaptation of J. K. Rowling's *Harry Potter and the Goblet of Fire*, the life of his character—doomed, handsome athlete, schoolboy, and all-around good guy, Cedric Diggory—was tragically cut short. Then, as dazzling Edward Cullen in the movie version of Stephenie Meyer's *Twilight*, he played another schoolboy, but this time one who can *never* die, and is eternally frozen at the age of seventeen, denying his dark nature for the sake of true love. What's the link? Both characters are exceedingly noble and outrageously crush worthy!

It's not just the characters that have something in common, either. *Twilight* also happens to be the most popular young-adult book since the Harry Potter series. So Robert Pattinson certainly owes a big thank-you to fans of both bestselling book series, since without the readers who love them, he might still be an unknown.

Not long before *Harry Potter and the Goblet of*

Fire was released, an interviewer met with Robert. At that time Triwizard champion Cedric was his biggest role to date. In between talking about his fellow actors and his band, Robert was asked what his next project would be. After all, what could possibly follow a global phenomenon like *Harry Potter*?

Robert tossed out several possibilities. He'd gotten his acting start in live theater productions, so he was considering returning to that. He also wanted to do something "weird." There had recently been a part he'd *really* wanted. The choice came down to him and one other guy—but the other guy got it. (Bet those casting directors are kicking themselves now!) Oh, and there was an American movie that he'd been offered, one that would involve him signing on for the possibility of at least three movies. . . .

At the time, fans had no idea that he was referring to *Twilight* and the successive possible movie sequels based on bestselling author Stephenie Meyer's Twilight

Saga. It's almost guaranteed that Robert had no idea how many fans the *Twilight* movie would have. But we're certainly glad that he said yes to that offer!

So how did a shy guy from a quiet London suburb end up as part of not one but two worldwide phenomena by the age of twenty-two? He has beautiful eyes and chiseled cheekbones, it's true, but he's also charming and talented—and he's a musician to boot! There's no doubt that Robert Pattinson is here to stay, and that's something to cheer about!

Rob's Dazzling Roots

**"Twelve was a turning point, as I moved
to a mixed school, and then I became cool
and discovered hair gel."**
—Robert Pattinson

Robert Thomas-Pattinson was born on May 13, 1986, in Barnes, a suburb of London, the capital of England. London has been a major settlement for over two thousand years, and is one of the world's leading centers for business, finance, and culture. It has a widely diverse population—more than three hundred languages are spoken in London. Robert grew up in an affluent and rather secluded area near the Thames

River, full of rich culture and elegant houses. And yes, we can thank his London upbringing for that a-maz-ing-ly sexy accent!

Lucky for Robert, two of his passions—music and theater—are significant influences in Barnes. The recording studio Olympic Studios, one of the town's prominent attractions, has hosted some of the biggest stars of pop and rock music, from the Beatles to Madonna to Coldplay. Another tourist site is the Old Sorting Office Arts Centre, which has become a key name in art and fringe theater. The Old Sorting Office hosts both art exhibits and theater productions, all open to the public. A teenage Robert played key roles in the Old Sorting Office's stage productions. After spending his early years in an area so supportive of the arts, it's no surprise that Robert has quickly risen to such heights in his acting career.

Robert is the youngest of three kids in the Pattinson family, and the only son. He has two older sisters. Elizabeth is three years older than he is, and Victoria is five years older. Robert's father, Richard, is a second-hand car dealer who specializes in importing vintage cars from America, and when Rob was growing up, his mother, Clare, worked for a modeling agency. Perhaps she's even the one who encouraged Rob to pursue the modeling he's done at various parts of his career.

Robert's dad loves that his son is involved in a creative profession. According to Robert: "My dad said to me the other day, 'I really am an artistic person.' I was shocked as I never saw him as creative. I think me and my sisters are living out that side of him as my sister is another creative person. She's a songwriter." Robert's sister Elizabeth, better known as Lizzy, has established herself in the music industry in England. Lizzy is both a singer and a songwriter. A scout from EMI, one of the "big four" major record labels, discovered her when she was seventeen. It seems that the Pattinson family's creative talents spring up strongly in their teenage years, because Robert, too, got his big break at age seventeen. In the

United Kingdom, Lizzy is the songwriting brains—
and often the onstage talent—behind a number of
bands that are known for hitting the top of the charts
with catchy pop tunes.

Lizzy has performed with the band Aurora UK,
which is a trio based in London. Lizzy's bandmates
are the keyboardist Simon Greenaway and guitarist
Sacha Collisson; Lizzy is the singer of the group. The
dance band's debut single was "Dreaming," and their
first album, released in 2002, was titled the same. In
fact, Lizzy can fill in her younger brother on the peaks
and pitfalls of skyrocketing fame, because by the time
she was eighteen, Aurora UK had had not one but
two Top Twenty hits: "Dreaming" and "The Day It
Rained Forever."

Aurora UK toured throughout the United Kingdom, North America, and Europe. They played in
many major music venues, and the concert crowds
often numbered more than 100,000 screaming fans!
Lizzy recently collaborated with Aurora UK again on

a 2006 song called "Summer Son." Aurora UK isn't the only band Lizzy Pattinson sings for, though. She's also worked with Milk & Sugar, singing "Let the Sunshine In," which hit the number one spot on the Billboard Dance Chart.

Robert and Lizzy's middle sister, Victoria, isn't involved in the music or theater world, but she channels the Pattinson creativity in another way, putting it to good use in her job in advertising. Unfortunately for Robert, his sisters' creativity wasn't always beneficial to him. "Up until I was twelve my sisters used to dress me up as a girl and introduce me as 'Claudia,'" he says. Growing up with two sisters might have had its pitfalls, but chances are it means Rob learned how to treat girls right early on. And anyway, "Twelve was a turning point, as I moved to a mixed school [a school with boys and girls], and then I became cool and discovered hair gel." Apparently trademark hair has been a part of Robert's persona ever since. At a press event promoting *Twilight*, a *Washington Post* reporter quizzed Robert on how he gets his artfully messy hair to stick up so perfectly. Robert laughed and said, "You just don't wash it. Ever."

Back to Robert's life history and the days in which he was first discovering hair gel . . . along with first discovering his talent for acting. The first school Robert attended was an all-boys school called the Tower House School. Tower House is located in a suburb close to Barnes, an area known for schools with high standards for excellence. Traditionally, a "tower house" could also be called a castle—a building built for either defense or for living in. The Tower House School is a preparatory school for boys ages four to thirteen. Music, art, and drama are considered a vital part of the Tower House School curriculum, and Robert got his first taste of acting while he was a student there. He began performing in school productions at age six. His roles included the King of Hearts (aww!) in a play written by one of the teachers called *Spell for a Rhyme* and Robert in William

Golding's *Lord of the Flies*.

"He wasn't a particularly academic child but he always loved drama," said Caroline Booth, a school secretary, to the *Evening Standard*. "He was an absolutely lovely boy, everyone adored him. We have lots of lovely boys here but he was something special. He was very pretty, beautiful and blond." Even back then, people appreciated Rob's talents—and his undeniable cuteness. Caroline Booth continued, "I wouldn't say he was a star but he was very keen on our drama club. We're all so pleased that he's found something he really shines at."

How else could his teachers and classmates tell that Robert was more interested in the theater than academics? Well, in a newsletter during his last year there, he was called "a runaway winner of last term's Form Three untidy desk award." Robert did serve as a lunch monitor at his school, but he wasn't always the best monitor, either. "I used to take everyone's chips!" he told the BBC. Not that this mischievous French fry thief wasn't ever the victim of pranks himself. "Someone stole my shoelaces once from my shoes," a younger Rob once revealed. "I still wear them and never put laces in them—they're like my trademark shoes now!" And even Robert acknowledges that he didn't have the best school reports. "They were always pretty bad—I never ever did my homework. I always turned up for lessons, as I liked my teachers, but my report said I didn't try very hard."

No question, Robert must have been a bit of a scoundrel, since he also admitted that he was expelled from school when he was twelve, though he wouldn't confess what, exactly, had caused that bit of drama! But his expulsion led to a change that Rob probably didn't mind all too much, after spending years with only other boys for classmates. The switch in schools meant that he started attending a co-ed school. And it seems he wasted no time getting to know some of those girls quite well, because he told *Seventeen* magazine that he had his first kiss at age twelve, too!

The Harrodian School was good for more than Rob's budding love life. It was a superb environment for a creative teenager. The school takes students—boys *and* girls—from ages four to eighteen and encourages them to reach their full potential, academically, physically, and socially. They also want their students to become well-rounded people who contribute positive things to the world. The curriculum at Harrodian encourages manners, consideration, and awareness of society and the world. It's not a large school, as the student body has fewer than one thousand students. But students there have lots of privileges. They have a heated outdoor swimming pool on the grounds for use in the summer and autumn terms, as well as science laboratories, a state-of-the-art computer lab, and a music and dramatic studies center.

American students might get a bit of culture shock if they attended the Harrodian School. The school's rules are certainly more strict than those we're used to here in the United States. Students there are expected to "line up quietly outside the classroom until told to enter by the teacher" and are not to have "graffiti" on their schoolbook covers. Leaving the school premises without permission can even result in "immediate expulsion"! And there's a very preppy dress code. While Robert attended the Harrodian School, he had to wear either gray or black trousers, a collared shirt and navy sweater, and dark socks and shoes. He wasn't allowed to wear hooded tops, sweaters with logos besides the school's, blue jeans or jean jackets, T-shirts under shirts, or athletic shoes. Boys aren't permitted to wear jewelry of any sort at Harrodian, and their haircuts can't be "extreme in style or length." (It's a good thing hair gel was still allowed.) On the plus side, though, all that emphasis on decorum creates a great reputation for the school. According to the school's website, "First-rate drama productions, art exhibitions, and musical events are features of Harrodian life, and a wide range of extra-curricular activities is offered each term."

Students at the Harrodian School are divided into four houses—just like at Hogwarts! The houses are named Bridge, Ferry, Lonsdale, and Thames, and each student is allocated a house when they enter the school. According to Harrodian's website: "Students are able to gain house points through Sport, Drama, Music, Public Speaking, Debating, and Citizenship." There's even the equivalent of the House Cup, though it has a slightly different name! Whichever house has the most points at the end of each term is presented with the Gallagher Shield. And, like Hogwarts, the school names a Head Boy and Head Girl each year, thought Robert never held that coveted title as his character Cedric did. Asked by the BBC who his favorite, most memorable teacher was, Robert replied, "Probably my English teacher because she got me into writing instead of just answering the question. I used to hand in homework with twenty pages of nonsense and she'd still mark it. She was a really amazing teacher." Robert has already proved two major creative talents—acting and music—perhaps someday we'll see his success as a writer, too.

Robert's teenage life wasn't all school, though. He was an active athlete, skiing, snowboarding, and playing soccer. He had a job, too. "I started doing a paper round when I was about ten," he said. "I started earning ten pounds [around twenty American dollars] a week and then I was obsessed with earning money until I was about fifteen." These days Robert has a much more sensible view of money. In an interview with music website virginmedia.com, he said he didn't want to look for a recording contract for his music until he felt absolutely ready. "My sister works so hard to make money and I think it ruins you," he concluded. Robert's business sense got him through the end of school, though, so it's good he has a level head for money matters. After he got his first screen acting job, he needed the income to pay for school. He told a London newspaper, the *Evening Standard*, "At the time, my father said to me, 'Okay, you might as well leave school now, since you're not working very hard.' And when I told him I wanted to stay on for my A levels, he said I'd have to pay my own fees—then he'd pay me back if I got good enough grades."

Wait! Is school optional in England?! Well, not completely, no. But the final two years of high school *are* optional. Students who complete those two years have to take Advanced levels (A levels)—a kind of super-intensive final exam. Many English universities consider the A levels an entrance examination—like the SATs or ACTs—requiring students to achieve a certain grade in order to be admitted. Often, A level classes—especially at small schools like Harrodian School—can be tiny. Robert's year had only six students! Unfortunately he didn't make good enough grades for his dad to pay him back. Remember that untidy desk award? Even though Robert wanted to complete his final two years, he quickly realized that he much preferred working in the theater to school. And since the same casting agent who helped him get that first screen part also helped him land the role of Cedric Diggory, Robert's focus on acting over academics paid off in the end.

We have Robert's dad to thank for his entrance into the acting world, though, so don't be too hard on him for not paying for those last two years of school. When asked how he became serious about acting, Robert responds, "My dad saw a bunch of pretty girls in a restaurant and he asked them where they came from and they said drama group. He said, 'Son, that is where you need to go.'" And it seems that suggestion was all the convincing that Robert needed. He was off to join the world of professional theater!

A Superstar Career Begins

"Sometimes I realize I could be working at a shoe shop. Acting is much cooler." —*Robert Pattinson*

At age fifteen, Robert joined the Barnes Theatre Company, a local performance group that produced two shows each year. This is certainly a case of Robert being in the right place at the right time; the Barnes Theatre Company is located just around the corner from the house he grew up in. Okay, maybe he *did* join thinking about the cute girls he might meet, at his dad's suggestion, but—potential girlfriends aside—he knew acting was something he enjoyed, and something that he had the potential to be quite good at. Robert told Scholastic, the American publisher of the Harry Potter books, "I really wasn't part of the acting fraternity at my school, but I joined this thing after my dad argued with me for ages. I think he had some sort of weird foresight about it." Sometimes it really does pay to listen to the parents—even when they're annoying.

Robert didn't leap right into acting lead roles, though. First he put in some time doing work backstage, which he admits was good for his somewhat oversize teenage ego. "I wasn't nervous of performing," he told *StageCoach Magazine*, "but at sixteen, I thought it would be arrogant [to admit that]!" In a local theater group, backstage work like Robert did could have included anything from helping to build and paint sets, to helping with costumes or changing furniture between scenes. Often, the backstage helpers are called techies because some create and run the technical aspects like lighting and sound. Most techies wear all black so that they are harder to see in the wings while a play is being performed. There's no way a hottie like Robert was going to blend into the crowd, though, and as he says, "For some reason when I finished the backstage thing, I just decided that I should try to act. So I auditioned for *Guys and Dolls*."

Guys and Dolls is a musical that was first produced in 1950, but has found lasting popularity as a choice for high schools and community theaters. It's about two high-stakes gamblers and the ladies they're in love with. The lead role is Nathan Detroit, a guy who's trying to find a new location for his illegal card-playing game. He makes a bet that another high-rolling gambler, Sky Masterson, can't get Sarah, the straitlaced lady in charge of the local missionary organization, to agree to a dinner date—in Havana, Cuba. With the typical crossed signals, mixed messages, laughter, and happy ending of a musical, Nathan and his on-again, off-again girlfriend, Adelaide, and the new couple, Sky and Sarah, fight, cry, make amends, and in the end profess their true love. *Guys and Dolls* received a Tony Award the first year it was on Broadway, and has been revived on Broadway, in the West End (London's version of Broadway), and in Australia. Robert, of course, was gunning for the lead, the role of Nathan Detroit, the same role that Frank Sinatra played in the movie version of *Guys and Dolls*. Disappointingly, though, he "got an embarrassing Cuban dancer part." Still, Robert showed his dedication to the company and to acting in general by giving the bit part his all. That paid off, because as Robert told *StageCoach*, "They respected me for doing it and gave me the lead in Thornton Wilder's *Our Town*—and that got me an agent."

It may be rather odd to think of *Our Town*, the quintessential American play, being produced in a small theater in England. But this may have been the first time Robert got to practice his American accent! *Our Town* is an older play than *Guys and Dolls*. It was first performed in 1938, and the American playwright Thornton Wilder won a Pulitzer Prize for writing it. *Our Town* tells the story of a small New England town called Grover's Corners, and of Emily Webb and George Gibbs, who fall in love as teenagers. The play is in three acts: the first showing a typical day in town, with Emily agreeing to help George with his homework; the second showing Emily and George's wedding day; and the third showing a sadder day— the day of Emily's funeral. Although the play has its sad moments, its main theme is to remind theater-goers to appreciate every second of even the most ordinary days. Robert played the lead role of George Gibbs, who has the strongest and most difficult emotional arc, and even as a teenager, Rob was surely up to that task.

Robert also starred in the Barnes Theatre Company's production of *Anything Goes*, a musical, also from the 1930s. *Anything Goes* is one of the famous musicals with music and lyrics by Cole Porter, and it debuted on

Broadway in 1934. It's been revived numerous times in both the United States and in the United Kingdom. There are two movie versions of it as well! Set on an ocean liner, with stowaways, star-crossed lovers, nightclub singers, public enemies, wealthy aristocrats, and heiresses, it's a story full of madcap antics. Robert played the role of Lord Evelyn Oakleigh, a stuffy and unlucky Englishman who ends up losing one fiancée and winning another. Come to think of it, after that first small dancing part in *Guys and Dolls*, in his key roles both onstage and on-screen, Rob has portrayed good-hearted guys seeking true love. It's no wonder we think he's the perfect guy!

Robert has nothing but positive things to say about his experience with the Barnes Theatre Company. He told scholastic.com, "They used to do two shows a year and they are all great. So many people from there had become actors. The directors were actors themselves and were very talented." He added, "I owe everything to that little club." We imagine that he's made his old directors quite proud of their former student, too!

The Barnes Theatre Company isn't the only local theater in his area of London, and Robert also found acting work from his mid-to-late teens with the Old Sorting Office Arts Centre. The Centre is a vital part of Barnes's social and cultural life. According to the Old Sorting Office's website, the OSO Arts Centre "provides a venue for theatre and live performances, art exhibitions, dance classes, music, drama for all ages and abilities, writers' groups, a film club, yoga, Pilates classes, education opportunities . . . , in fact, anything and everything." The stage manager who worked at OSO throughout Robert's years there remembers him well as a "smashing kid." She confirms what Robert now freely admits, saying, "I think he only joined because of the girls!" She went on to mention that Rob still goes back to visit his old OSO friends when he's in England and "is always welcome." And she says that it's been rewarding to follow Robert's career since he left the OSO, remarking, "It's quite lovely to see that he's gone on to do so well." Sounds like everyone who knew Robert in his younger years is delighted to know about the success that this budding star is finding.

At the Old Sorting Office, Robert won the role of Malcolm in Shakespeare's stage classic *Macbeth*. This is a tragic play: Macbeth, an honored soldier in Scotland, grows so power hungry that he and his wife conspire to murder the king in order to place Macbeth on the throne. Malcolm is the true king's son, who flees Macbeth's greed, but eventually returns to take the throne and reestablish order in the kingdom. In other words, this, too, was a fitting, noble role for the young man who has now become a symbol of nobility because of his role as a "vegetarian" vampire.

But though it's nice to get the girl and be the noble hero most of the time, Robert likes playing the bad guy every now and then, too! The first time he did this was also his first true period role—as Alec in the

OSO's production of *Tess of the D'Urbervilles*. The play is based on a Victorian novel by Thomas Hardy, published in 1891. *Tess* is a tragic drama about a young peasant woman whose family tries to force her to marry someone well-off to bring them better circumstances. Alec, the young man whom Robert played, is an unsavory character—a big difference from those three previous roles. While he probably didn't get to twirl a villainous mustache or perfect a dastardly laugh, this role gave him his first experience in playing a death scene, something he could call on for his later role as doomed Cedric Diggory in *Harry Potter*.

From the live stage to the big screen wasn't too giant a leap for Robert. It was clear to anyone who saw him perform that he'd been bitten by the acting bug, and that he might just have what it takes to make it on-screen. Robert's first film role was in a German made-for-television movie called *Ring of the Nibelungs*, which aired in 2004. The story is based on the Germanic and Nordic legends that inspired J. R. R. Tolkien's *Lord of the Rings,* as well as the composer Richard Wagner's famed Ring Cycle operas. In *Ring of the Nibelungs,* a young blacksmith named Siegfried, who doesn't know he's actually heir to a kingdom, slays a dragon and accepts a cursed hoard of gold as his reward.

Robert was just seventeen at the time that he played a small part as Giselher, a king's son. *Ring of the Nibelungs* filmed in Cape Town, South Africa. Robert told virginmedia.com, "I was there for three months in an apartment at just seventeen! So I came back really confident." *Ring of the Nibelungs* is called *Dark Kingdom: The Dragon King* here in the United States. The movie was Robert's first time with filming special effects, which, he said, "are probably one of the strangest things to go into if you have never done acting before." It's a good thing that he got experience working with special effects on this smaller scale, because he would soon have much more intense special effects to act with in *Harry Potter* and *Twilight.* After all, it's not in every film that an actor plays a part that involves running across treetops and making his skin sparkle like diamonds!

The year 2004 was a busy one for Rob. Besides the role in *Ring of the Nibelungs*, he also filmed a small part in the major film *Vanity Fair*, which starred Reese Witherspoon as a social-climbing antiheroine named Becky Sharp. Another Victorian period piece, *Vanity Fair* is an adaptation of the 1847 novel by William Makepeace Thackeray. Robert's role was Becky's grown son, Rawdy Crawley. Sadly for Robert's fans seeking that footage, his scenes were cut from the theatrical version of the film—but some are available in the DVD extras.

Robert's best friend, Tom Sturridge, also had a small part in *Vanity Fair*. Tom and Robert had met through Tom's siblings, who attended the Harrodian School with Robert. The two guys have been friends for years and are often photographed out on the town together, enjoying each other's company, comparing notes on movie work, and likely reminiscing about all the trouble they got into together during their shared school days.

Besides acting, Robert did some modeling work in his late teens and early twenties as well—no surprise there, given his dashing good looks and killer smile (not to mention that über-sexy, just-rolled-out-of-bed hair)! He modeled at times under the more formal name of Robert Thomas-Pattinson, perhaps to distinguish the modeling from his rapidly growing acting résumé. His most widely seen campaign was for the British clothing label Hackett. Robert, along with fellow heartthrobs Matthew Goode and Jamie Strachan, was selected for Hackett's Autumn/Winter 2007 line, and wise choices they all were. Hackett, according to its website, "is a classic British clothing and accessories brand which caters for the head to toe needs of men of all ages who wish to dress stylishly and to whom quality is more important than the vagaries of fashion." In other words, Hackett aims to represent the tradition of British clothing without being old-fashioned.

A peek at the Hackett website (or a search online for Rob's shots from the advertising campaign) reveals just the sort of impeccably groomed, timeless attire that pops to mind with the words, "British gentleman." And with classically good-looking men like Robert Pattinson wearing the clothes, how can they look anything but dashing? Robert talks very little about his modeling stints, but that's why they say a picture is worth a thousand words!

Has Robert ever wondered what he might have been doing in those years between school and his casting as Cedric Diggory if he hadn't listened to his dad and tried acting? Scholastic asked just that question in an interview, and Robert responded, "I have no idea. I was thinking about that. I would have just gone to university and would have kind of just done the average thing." If Robert had chosen to do the "average thing," he would have applied to a university after completing his A levels in high school. Students in England get to choose which subjects they'd like to study for the A levels, and often that's what they go on to concentrate on in the university. Most British students earn their bachelor's degree in only three years, and tuitions for many schools are government funded to keep costs low for the students. Even still, Rob has his days where he feels less than confident, or when the pressures of his career get overwhelming. "Sometimes I think, 'To hell with acting.'" Luckily for all his fans, he usually snaps out of those funks pretty quickly. "And then I realize I could be working at a shoe shop. Acting is much cooler."

Rob is quick to recognize his incredible good fortune. "I was just talking to my agent about that the other day," Robert continued. "It is unbelievable that this stroke of luck has completely changed my entire life. I can't even remember what I was thinking those two years ago. Now I sort of do things differently, and I am reading all these scripts. I was out in LA a couple of weeks ago. I got an agent in LA, and it is ridiculous." But it's not so ridiculous to anyone who's seen Robert's talented performances. So it looks like fans can add "humble" to the long list of admirable traits that make him dreamy!

Breakthrough!
Rob's Champion Role

**"Everyone semi-idolizes Cedric.
All the girls fancy him, and the guys
want to be him."** —*Robert Pattinson*

The leading roles with the Barnes Theatre Company
and the Old Sorting Office Arts Centre were great
parts for Robert to cut his teeth on. They led to
finding his agent and landing the small parts in the
television movies and in *Vanity Fair*. But in 2003 came
the critical moment in Robert's career: the audition for
Harry Potter and the Goblet of Fire.

Pretty much anyone who hasn't been living under

a rock for the last ten years knows about *Harry Potter*. The Harry Potter franchise is one of the largest book and movie franchises in the world. It all began in 1998 with the book *Harry Potter and the Sorcerer's Stone* by J. K. Rowling, and the seventh and final book of the series, *Harry Potter and the Deathly Hallows*, was published in 2007. As of June 2008, the series had sold more than 400 million copies worldwide. It has been translated into sixty-seven languages—including "dead" languages like Latin! The world had never seen a far-reaching publishing phenomenon quite like Harry Potter. Fans span all ages, from elementary school kids to teenagers, to parents, and even grandparents. The last three books in the series were released with great fanfare at midnight parties around the globe. Now each book of the series, except for the final one, has been made into a blockbuster movie, full of special effects and amazing actors—including the one and only Robert Pattinson, of course.

In 2003, when Robert was seventeen, the long-awaited fifth book, *Harry Potter and the Order of the Phoenix*, had finally been published, and movies of the first two books, *Harry Potter and the Sorcerer's Stone* and *Harry Potter and the Chamber of Secrets*, had become smash hits. The third movie was in production, and the movie executives were already looking ahead to the fourth, *Harry Potter and the Goblet of Fire*. The same casting agent who suggested Robert for *Vanity Fair* suggested him for *Goblet of Fire*.

As it turns out, Rob may have been among the very few people who had still not read a single Harry Potter book, and he quickly read *Goblet of Fire* before auditioning. ("I've read three and five now as well, and I'm halfway through six!" he claims.) The day before Robert was to leave for South Africa to film *Ring of the Nibelungs*, the casting agent introduced him to Mike Newell, the director of *Goblet of Fire*. "I was the first person to be seen for any part on the film, which could have helped," Robert said. But that doesn't mean he was confident he'd gotten the part at the time! "I am now determined to do really weird parts," he continued, "but I think I overdo it in auditions so nobody really trusts me!"

Robert took off for Cape Town, South Africa, and spent three months filming *Ring of the Nibelungs*. The day he came back from that adventure, he had his callback for *Goblet of Fire* and embarked on an adventure even more remarkable. He met again with Mike Newell, who told him after the audition that he'd earned the role of Triwizard Champion Cedric Diggory. As he said to Virgin Media just before *Goblet of Fire* hit theaters, "Since I started acting it's kind of been a bit mad. I never really did anything before and two years ago I started acting and I've kind of been in work ever since. Then *Harry Potter* came along and it's been a huge step and a massive event in my life." But even Robert couldn't have possibly imagined the charmed acting life that the role of Cedric Diggory would open for him.

The plot of *Harry Potter and the Goblet of Fire*

hinges on the Triwizard Tournament, an international competition that takes place at Hogwarts School of Witchcraft and Wizardry. Two other wizard schools, Beauxbatons and Durmstrang, send their students to Hogwarts, and a champion is chosen from each to compete in three challenges throughout the academic year. Cedric Diggory is the official Hogwarts Champion—the home team favorite, if you will. Cedric is seventeen years old (the same age as Robert was during filming) and in his final year at Hogwarts. He is a part of the Hufflepuff house and, like all Hufflepuffs, is known for his dedication and hard work. But he's not just any Hufflepuff—Cedric is Head Boy, the designated representative and leader of his entire class. He is also a Quidditch player, and is one of the only Quidditch Seekers to have bested Harry during a Quidditch match.

When Robert was asked what his first impressions of the character of Cedric were, he responded, "I think he's a pretty cool character." It would be practically impossible not to like a guy like Cedric! Robert added insight to his breakout role, though, explaining, "He's not really a complete cliché of the good kid in school. He's just quiet. He is actually just a genuinely good person, but he doesn't make a big deal about it or anything. I can kind of relate to that. He's not an unattractive character at all and his story line is a nice story line to play." Discovering the nuances and different sides of a character is part of the challenge of acting, and Robert rose to the task here, finding more depth to Cedric than just being an all-around nice guy.

Cedric wants to win the Triwizard Cup and to beat Harry, who was added to the tournament as a fourth champion (and second representative of Hogwarts) through a series of peculiar events. But despite his ambition, Cedric never fights dirty. "It's impossible to hate Cedric. He's competitive but he's also a nice guy," says Robert. "Everyone semi-idolizes him. All the girls fancy him, and the guys want to be him." That's quite a tall order. Was Robert a perfect fit for such an upstanding young gentleman? According to director Mike Newell, he definitely was! "Cedric exemplifies all that you would expect the Hogwarts champion to be," Newell told the *Evening Standard*. "Robert Pattinson was born to play the role; he's quintessentially English with chiselled public schoolboy good looks."

But does Robert himself think that he's just like Cedric? It may be hard to believe, but no, he doesn't. "Not at all," he told the *Evening Standard*. "I was never a leader, and the idea of my ever being made head boy would have been a complete joke. I wasn't involved in much at school, and I was never picked for any of the teams." Playing a character he sees as quite different from himself gave Robert some new perspectives. He said during a Japanese interview, "Cedric is a really polite guy, and I wasn't really before. I became a lot more polite during the filming and I started holding open doors for people and things. And saying thank you for everything. People would say hello to me, and I would say thank you back." Holding doors open, being über-polite—*oooh la la!* If it's possible, playing the heroic Cedric Diggory made Robert even more attractive, so for that we say, "Thank you, J. K. Rowling!"

Playing Cedric was Robert's largest role to that point, but he didn't let it go to his seventeen-year-old head. Being in *Goblet of Fire* meant acting alongside some of the greatest adult actors working in Britain today, from Ralph Fiennes to Michael Gambon to Maggie Smith and more. It must have been daunting for many of the new cast members to consider. When asked if he found himself at all starstruck during his work on the movie, Robert replied, "Yeah, I did. I'm a big fan of Michael Gambon. They were all really, really nice people and they treat it as a job. They don't really have big egos or anything about it. There was one guy—Warwick Davis—he's in *Willow,* and *Willow* is like my favorite film." Can you imagine working with someone who starred in your favorite film? Robert was speechless at the experience. "I had one scene sitting next to [Warwick Davis] at the dragon task, and I had no idea what to say to him at all!" he said. "He was the only person I asked for an autograph the whole way through it!"

Being in the presence of so many experienced, renowned actors pushed Robert to do his absolute best. "I really wanted to do it really well because I'm still young and a relatively inexperienced actor," he explained quite earnestly. He funneled his nervousness into his preparation for the part, rather than sitting around fretting about it. As he told one interviewer, "I put quite a lot of work into it in the beginning. So I ignored all my nerves by sitting and looking at the script or reading the book ten times." Reading a 752-page book ten times over? Anyone would say that kind of dedication *more* than makes up for his having only read the book once before the audition!

Preparing to play Cedric Diggory wasn't just a matter of finding all of Cedric's layers or knowing the book backward and forward. Robert also had to face catapulting into the public eye as an immediate heart-throb. Not only did Robert have to do his best acting work to keep up with the legends he was working with, but he had to deal with the pressure of always looking perfect—never getting a zit or having a bad hair day (not that we actually believe that Rob could *ever* have one of those). Asked how he felt about playing such a dreamy guy, Robert answered, "That is quite difficult. In the book and also my first intro-duction of the script is like 'an absurdly handsome seventeen-year-old' and it kind of puts you off a little bit, when you're trying to act, and you're trying to get good angles to look good-looking and stuff. It's really stupid; you'd think I'm really egotistical. But I think that's the most daunting part about it—it's much scar-ier than meeting Voldemort!" Still, he wasn't entirely comfortable with one label as he gained notice for *Harry Potter and the Goblet of Fire.* "I read the *Variety* review and their only comment was 'rangy,'" he said. "I thought it meant from the range, like a cowboy.

But it just means tall and lanky." Now, modesty is an endearing quality, but we think that comment was just a moment of absurdity for Robert-slash-Cedric. Because who could ever think a hottie like Robert Pattinson is *just* tall?

Magic

"I wanted to be taken really seriously as an actor so I used to just sit around just drinking coffee all day and trying to look really intense." —*Robert Pattinson*

So what were Robert's days on the *Goblet of Fire* set like? As a new cast member joining an already tight-knit team of actors, there were sure to be some adjustments and challenges for all the actors involved. After all, the main actors had worked together on the previous Harry Potter movies and had a deep understanding of one another's working styles, as well as their personalities on and off the set. The new actors were totally outside that loop. Luckily Robert bonded quickly with two of the other new actors, whom he still counts among his close friends today—Katie Leung, who played Cedric's girlfriend, Cho Chang, and Stanislav Ianevski, who played fellow Triwizard competitor Viktor Krum. In fact, there's a hilarious clip of Robert enthusiastically hugging—er, *male bonding with*—his new pal Stan on their shared first day on set. (Just search YouTube for "Robert Pattinson hugs Krum," or look for it on the DVD extras . . . and get ready to say "awww!")

The instant camaraderie between the new actors was a fantastic bonus, but the movie's makers already had plans in place to ensure that Rob and his fellow newbies—like the other Triwizard champions—would fit right into the Harry Potter family. The shoot, which would last nearly a year, began on March 21, 2004, but Mike Newell, the movie's director, decided to have the young members of his cast meet before that. "We had two weeks of acting classes, and the reason that we did this was that I was very anxious that the established characters would not dominate the newcomers, many of whom had never acted before," Newell said in a *Goblet of Fire* press conference. "What we did was we played. We did physical exercises, we did improvisation exercises, and so on and so forth. And by the end of that, everybody was loose in one another's company." And it worked! The two weeks were invaluable for the cast, both new and old. Robert often paired with Rupert Grint, aka Ron Weasley, during the bonding camp and found Rupert just as funny in real life as his character. Robert said, "I didn't notice the transition to being accepted, but they are all really nice people. It seems like it should have been daunting but it wasn't."

That's not to say that everything was smooth sailing the whole time, though. Most of the maze scenes were scheduled to shoot in the early days of filming. Those scenes involved just him and Daniel Radcliffe, who plays Harry Potter. Daniel is a few years younger than Robert, and still had to spend five hours of every day in "school," working with a tutor on set. Rob had already finished with school (even the dreaded A levels). "I was just sitting by myself for ages," Robert said, "and at the time I wanted to be taken really seriously as an actor so I used to just sit around just drinking coffee all day and trying to look really intense." Looking intense probably wasn't too hard for Rob, not with those incredible eyes. . . .

The role of Cedric was physically demanding as well as mentally and emotionally challenging. Although Robert is an active young man (how else could he stay looking so fine?), being a Triwizard champion required more than simply being athletic. "It's a very physical part. The stuff in the maze, which was done in the beginning, was all on huge action sets," Robert told Virgin Media. "The hedges were huge and hydraulically operated. I got hit by stuff, getting pulled around by ropes, and Dan and I were running around punching each other so it was kind of vicious!"

Since the first two weeks of the shoot were just

Robert and Daniel in the maze—which was the final task of the Triwizard Tournament—he had to jump right into the most physical part of the shoot for him. Luckily he thoroughly enjoyed it! "The maze was really fun. A lot of the stunts are very contrived, and someone's practiced them a hundred times and you have to get it perfect otherwise it's pointless doing it. You're not gonna be in the right shot or anything. But in the maze, a lot of it was on Steadicam—which is just a guy running around with a camera." Sound too complicated and technical to picture clearly, even if you've seen the movie? Here's what it boils down to, in regular guy-speak: "Me and Dan were basically chasing each other around and punching each other, with these hedges squeezing us. And the camera would just follow you around, so you could basically do whatever you wanted. It was really fun. There were lots of cuts and bruises afterwards and it felt like you were doing a proper job!"

These male-bonding scenes continued to build on

the camaraderie that the cast had formed during their week of improvisation workshops. Robert felt confident in saying that those tournament filming scenes would have been a lot harder if it wasn't for director Mike Newell. He told one interviewer that it was the director who "came up with the idea that in the maze it is just the fear and the darkness and the isolation that kind of drives all the competitors a bit insane. We were really hyped up. You are on 100 percent adrenaline and you're starting this in the first week and you have just met all the other actors the week before and now you have to go crazy with them." The weeks of bonding before shooting allowed Robert and the other actors to reach a level of openness and connection necessary to produce such intense acting experiences.

Running and fighting weren't the only sports the actors had to excel in. They also had to master swimming on-screen, which is a lot trickier than simply swimming in a pool, as Robert is quick to tell anyone who asks. He spent approximately two months on the underwater scenes, which are a major part of the second task of the tournament. He had to take three weeks of scuba diving lessons before shooting those scenes. "There was a lot of underwater stuff which I quite liked, it got therapeutic after a while. I had never scuba dived before and the tank they taught us in was a little bathtub. The real thing was massive, like sixty feet deep and they expect you to just get in and act." Just imagine having to act without being able to breathe!

Even though he spent so much time learning the proper way to scuba dive, doing so in a bathtub-sized pool with lots of gear on and in a sixty-foot tank are like two different worlds. Robert had to swim underwater holding his breath, and then take "hits" of oxygen from divers in the tank with him. "On the first day of shooting in the tank, you have to hold your breath and there's nothing there!" Robert said. "There were a couple of times where you think you're swimming towards a guy with a breathing apparatus and then you find it's just some thing in the water," he said, and of course, not finding the oxygen made him freak out for a moment until he realized what to do. But alas, the cameras didn't stop rolling during that momentary panic. "They film your stupid face just screaming underwater, and then everyone starts laughing and it's just like, ahh, great!" Too bad those outtakes never made it to YouTube or the DVD extras, because Robert's "stupid face" is undoubtedly still completely heart melting. But it's a great example of Rob's good-natured spirit, which, along with his sense of humor, his ability to laugh at himself, and his willingness to throw himself so wholeheartedly into every single thing that he does, seems to make him stand out on every set, even in the everyday sort of moments.

Those key qualities are ones that many of the actors in *Goblet of Fire* shared, as working with action and special effects requires leaving dignity aside every once in a while. In an interview with *Disney Adventures* magazine, Robert mentioned how hard it was to dive heroically. "We had to do this scene looking like heroes diving into the lake. They had a stand-in doing perfect dives on the first take. Then Stan, Clémence, and I tried, but none of us could dive in right, and we all looked really stupid." Robert is sure the water scenes were the hardest part of filming *Goblet of Fire*, but in the end he found it quite calming. "You'd really concentrate on what you're supposed to be doing," he told a BBC interviewer. "You can't talk to anyone so you stay completely in character. You can't see anything so all you can hear is your director through the water, saying like 'look scared.' It was pretty fun. It was really fun!"

Keep in mind that this was Robert's first large film role. Though *Ring of the Nibelungs* included some special effects and action, a large-budget film like *Harry Potter and the Goblet of Fire* far outstrips what's possible on a made-for-television movie or even a film like *Vanity Fair*. "It was amazing. It was a very different thing to anything I've ever experienced," he said.

Nothing can compare to *Harry Potter*, especially for a modest young man who had just begun his film career. "The scale of Harry Potter is huge, people have been working on it for four or five years. There are two thousand people working on the set—not many films can afford that kind of 'epic-ness,'" he told Virgin Media.

Though it was like nothing Robert had done before, he wasn't about to let his amateur status or inexperience detract from his performance—even if he had to fib just a little to get the part in the first place. "I could barely swim before, but I told them in the audition that I could." Then again, who wouldn't tell a *tiny* little white lie in order to get a chance to break through like Robert did? And he might have gotten his comeuppance later, what with all those scuba-diving freak-outs caught on tape.

Just because Robert hadn't done much swimming before didn't mean he wasn't up to the challenge, and once he got the job, he made getting up to speed in that area a big priority. He quickly learned, though, that fitness drills aren't really his idea of fun. "I had to do a lot of fitness regimes and things in the beginning," he said in an interview with *Film Review* magazine. "I thought that would be pretty cool, because it would make me take it seriously. It was run by one of the stunt team, who are the most absurdly fit guys in the world. I can't even do ten press ups." For an active skier and snowboarder like Robert, the "regime" part of "fitness regime" wasn't the ideal exercise situation. "I did about three weeks of that, and in the end I think [the trainer] got so bored of trying to force me to do it that he wrote it all down so that I could do it at home." This worked out much better for both of them: Robert was able to keep in shape without getting bored, and his trainer didn't have to nag and pester him to do it. Most important of all, he was able to turn in a polished performance fighting his way through the maze with Daniel Radcliffe, swimming his way through the second task, and dealing with all of the other intensely physical moments of the Tri-wizard Tournament.

The less athletic scenes were sometimes a different story, though. The Yule Ball is the closest Hogwarts gets to having a prom, and it was a significant moment in the film. In one scene leading up to the ball, the stern Professor McGonagall teaches the students how to dance formally, and none of the guys are at all thrilled about learning this particular skill. Those weren't hard sentiments to act—the dancing scenes *were* a challenge. And since Robert never had a prom at his high school—there were only six students in his class!—he wasn't necessarily looking forward to this part of filming. "I think the Yule Ball is more attractive to the girls who read it," he said. "I never really thought 'Oh, I get to go to the ball!'" We can't expect even a hottie like Rob to be more excited by the scenes involving pretty gowns and dancing than the ones involving fear, fighting, and death around every corner, can we?

To properly prepare for the ballroom scene, all of the cast members involved in the Yule Ball had to take part in a choreography session that lasted two weeks. They learned the waltz, among other dances, and how to coordinate themselves while dancing as a large group, but only a few small bits of those lessons wound up being in the final cut of the movie. Even with all the dancing, "That was a really fun period," Robert told fans and reporters in a pre-movie press release with Katie Leung (Cho Chang) and Stanislav Ianevski (Viktor Krum). "Because I've never really done Renaissance . . . Is it Renaissance or a waltz? Some classical dancing. I really think I learned a lot."

Much to everyone's surprise, the classical dancing made them feel *less* self-conscious than the unchoreographed dancing scenes, like the dancing that happens to any fast song at a normal high school dance. Because "regular" dancing doesn't involve any standard moves, or strict choreography, Robert felt that it was harder—and it definitely made him more self-conscious—than waltzing. "I think the most embarrassing part of that was just the normal dancing. When the rock band comes. I think there was two days where the crew was like, 'Just dance, just dance.' That was really awkward," he told the press conference.

Robert also has the first major death scene in any of the Harry Potter movies. In the final Triwizard Tournament task, Harry and Cedric decide to share the prize, but instead of ending the tournament in glory, they are transported to a dark graveyard where the evil Lord Voldemort is waiting to return to his full power. Cedric is callously disposed of moments after their arrival in the graveyard with the killing curse Avada Kedavra, when Voldemort says to "Kill the spare." In 2008, *Entertainment Weekly* ranked this scene as number four in their "Twenty-five New Classic Death Scenes" list. They wrote, "Number Four: The murder of kind and decent Cedric Diggory. It's the darkest moment up to that point in the Potter saga, as

Harry experiences the death of someone close to him for the first time since he lost his parents. Meanwhile, he's forced to confront just how deadly his nemesis Voldemort is, and how likely it is that their clash may claim the lives of more innocents."

A good death scene can be something actors wait years to land, but Robert got his in his very first blockbuster role! Rather than agonizing over how dramatic or understated to play it, he took it all in stride, as any true professional would, and joked about the experience to reporters in between the rehearsals of the scene and its actual filming. "Well, I haven't actually died 'live' yet but I've been dead a few times. It's strange, but it's quite sort of relaxing. You feel like a bit of a therapist, because everyone's giving you all their grief, and you're just lying there listening. Yeah, it was quite nice, like no pressure after a couple weeks. I enjoyed it."

Though no day on a film set can truly be described as typical, Robert was kind enough to give fans a good idea of what shooting *Goblet of Fire* was like for him in the pre-release press conference with Katie and Stan. "There wasn't anything of any sort of structure," he said. "There would be days where hardly anything would happen, where you'd stand around the whole time because it was such a long shoot. Everything was shooting for about eleven months or something in total, so there were days and weeks where you would do absolutely nothing."

Generally Robert would have to be on set at six thirty in the morning. (Ack! That's too early!) In an interview on the *Goblet of Fire* DVD, Clémence Poésy (Fleur Delacour) said if actors arrived late to set, then they wouldn't have time to eat before they needed to be in hair and makeup. If Robert arrived at his usual six thirty, he'd be able to eat breakfast, then have his hair and makeup done, get into costume, and start work around nine. "Some days were just ridiculously busy while other days, especially when there is stunt work or something like that, [there was] a lot of time waiting around," he said in the press conference. Regardless of the early mornings and the unpredictable schedule, Robert would never complain about his time on the *Goblet of Fire* set. When the BBC asked him if there were any "bad parts" about shooting the film, Robert's answer was an unequivocal "No!" He said, "It was a really long shoot so it was kinda tiring by the end, but all in all it was really fun, and there were a lot of amazing periods, which was really nice."

More than Just a Pretty Face

"He's a beautiful musician, a very creative soul, very similar to Edward."

—*Catherine Hardwicke*

Edward Cullen is the quintessential hot hero to Twi-lighters around the world, but who is Robert Pattinson's hero? Well, Robert has said he'd love to play Gambit from *X-Men.* And when the *Los Angeles Times* asked him which superhero he'd like to play, he claimed Spider-Man would be cool—for a slightly surprising reason: "I like the outfit; I like a little bit of spandex." And who wouldn't like to see Robert *in* a little spandex? Hopefully studio heads are taking note and picturing

Robert as the next big comic book superhero on the docket, because his fans certainly now are!

In all seriousness, Robert admires many of the great actors in the generations before him. For the role of Edward, he drew on a number of iconic performances. "There are bits of *Rebel Without a Cause* and stuff," he said to joblo.com, referring to the great young movie star of the fifties, James Dean. Performances such as Dean's helped him get an initial handle on a character who is very much a loner and endlessly complex. Edward is Robert's first film role with an American accent. Luckily he didn't find it to be too much of a challenge. When MTV asked how he went about learning to mimic one, he said, "I grew up watching American movies and stuff, so I've learned how to 'act' from American films." There's not necessarily a particular actor that he modeled the accent after, though, unless it was by accident. "At the beginning, when I was doing the first couple scenes, I kept slipping into different actors," he said. Then he laughed, and added, "During a really dramatic scene, you start doing Al Pacino."

As far as vampire inspiration goes, Robert names Gary Oldman as one of his favorite movie vampires. Oldman played Count Dracula in the 1992 movie adaptation of Bram Stoker's novel *Dracula*. "I also like the actor in the original *Nosferatu*. He's amazing. I mean, he has an amazing face. I thought he was really cool," he continued. *Nosferatu* is a very old silent film. Made in Germany in 1922, before movies had sound, it starred Max Schreck as the villainous vampire. Clearly, when Robert decides to research roles, he takes it seriously! To him, taking in the classics of the vampire movie genre is just as essential as reading the entire Twilight Saga in order to fully formulate and "become" his idea of Edward.

The actor that Robert most admires has never played a vampire—Jack Nicholson. He admits that as a young teen, he felt a bit of hero worship for the legendary actor. He said in an interview, "I aspire to be

Jack Nicholson. I love every single mannerism. I used to try and be him in virtually everything I did, I don't know why. I watched *One Flew Over the Cuckoo's Nest* when I was about thirteen, and I dressed like him. I tried to do his accent. I did everything like him. I think it's kind of stuck with me." Jack Nicholson is one of the most acclaimed actors in American film, with a broad range of roles in his repertoire, and he has collected awards for a variety of nuanced and subtle roles, as well as more over-the-top ones. So a career like his is definitely a worthy aspiration for a young actor shooting to fame.

In the same way, Robert has made varied choices that have led to not only blockbuster, much-hyped roles, such as Cedric Diggory and Edward Cullen, but also roles in independent films like *How to Be* and *Little Ashes*, so his dream of being like Jack Nicholson is on track so far.

Jack Nicholson is even the inspiration for Robert's stage name as a musician: Bobby Dupea. Bobby Dupea is the main character (played by Nicholson, of course) in the 1970 movie *Five Easy Pieces*. In the movie, Bobby is a gifted concert pianist who comes from a well-off family of musicians. But he is a restless and sometimes angry young man; so to escape the dull, sheltered routine of practice and performance, he takes off on the road to see the world. Eventually, though, he does reunite with his family, having experienced many important moments that allowed him to come to know himself as a more well-rounded human being. So why is this the name that Rob chose as his "incognito" cover as a musician? Well, there's the obvious Robert-Bobby link, and there's a clear tip of the hat to Jack Nicholson, too. Perhaps Robert even sometimes dreams of running away from his ever-growing fame to "see the world." But the deepest reason of all may be one that *Seventeen* magazine got him to admit . . . that his dream job is being a pianist—just like Bobby Dupea in *Five Easy Pieces*!

Music has been a large part of Robert's world from

a very young age, partly because of his sister's success. He's seen that it takes a lot of work and dedication, but that it's actually a career in which it's possible to have great success. Having watched his sister's interests develop, the tremendously creative Robert had to try his hand at music, too. Just as *Goblet of Fire* was hitting the screens around the world, he told *Movie Magic*, "I have been playing the piano for my entire life—since I was three or four. And the guitar—I used to play classical guitar from when I was about five to twelve years of age. Then I didn't play guitar for like years. About four or five years ago, I got out the guitar again and just started playing blues and stuff. I am not very good at the guitar, but I am all right. I am in a band in London as well." That band was called Bad Girls, and was started by his first girlfriend's then-current boyfriend. How's that for awkward! Perhaps it's not surprising that Robert is no longer with that band.

The band he's with now is unnamed, or at least he

wouldn't admit its name to a persistent fan who asked about it during a signing at a convention. But he did say that they play gigs in London and did a festival in Wales. So who knows? Maybe one day if you're in London, you'll run into Robert and his mates jamming out in the most unexpected of spots!

What legendary musicians does Robert love? Who is his Jack Nicholson equivalent in the music world? Funnily enough, when Robert was in junior high, his musical heroes were Eminem and Jay Kay from Jamiroquai, since he was "really into rap" at that time, he told the BBC. These days, his music is much more low-key. He likes blues and country-inspired rock. His sound is folksy and almost Bob Dylan–like—he, too, can play the guitar and the harmonica at the same time.

Could a career in music lure Robert away from acting entirely? It's possible, but if so, then landing the role as Edward may have recharged both his acting career and—unexpectedly—his musical aspirations.

In the novel, Edward is a gifted pianist. (Are we sensing a theme?) After all, it's not like he has a whole lot to do during long nights, since vampires in Stephenie Meyer's universe don't need sleep. *Twilight* is chock-full of achingly romantic scenes between Bella and Edward, but the most heart-melting scene of all may be when Edward sits down at the beautiful grand piano in his home and plays the song he has composed for Bella. What does this song sound like? It's the question that Twihards everywhere are dying to know the answer to. And since Robert was cast as Edward and the great "Is he hot enough?" debate was laid to rest—at least by most—it may be the next biggest question that fans have devoted themselves to pondering.

Everyone has an idea of what the song *should* sound like, and fans have been unafraid to lobby their selections to Stephenie and the *Twilight* director, Catherine Hardwicke. Many suspected it would be a reinterpretation of one of the songs on Stephenie's

Twilight-inspired list, or maybe even an original composition by her favorite band, Muse. When he signed on for the part, musical ability wasn't on the checklist of necessary attributes, so no one involved in the movie anticipated that Robert himself might pen the all-important song. That he ended up doing so was a dream come true, both for the moviemakers and the waiting fans! But that's exactly what happened, and now it seems the most obvious possibility of all.

After all, Robert had kept up with his music while on the *Twilight* set. Like most musicians, his music is deeply rooted, a part of his soul, and a key to his creative process. And like any passionate person, he is driven to do the things that feed him creatively, and for Rob, that thing is making music. So it's not something Rob could just quit doing during the months of filming. It's not at all surprising, then, that he found ways to satisfy his musical urges while on set, filling up off-set moments and allowing him to diffuse some of the stresses of playing the intense character of Edward. "I was doing music before I started acting," Robert said, "so I still have bits and pieces, and I've been playing in Portland [during the shoot]." But his music playing and writing couldn't be contained by impromptu offstage performances. He revealed to MTV, "The lullaby thing, I just made [it] up on the spot during the scene. During the scene, I drifted into the piano playing. I guess it just comes from somewhere." And director Catherine Hardwicke, a wildly creative and artistic soul herself, recognizes genius when she sees it.

Catherine cast Robert as Edward in the first place, knowing that no one else would be as perfect in the role, and it's clear that she's as delighted with his musical ability as with his acting ability. "He's a beautiful musician, a very creative soul, very similar to Edward. He just totally reads the most interesting stuff, and sees the most interesting movies, and is very introspective and diving into his existential self," she said. So when it came time for "Bella's Lullaby" to be created, she gave him free rein to see what he could do. "I told him he should write one, and let's see if we can make it work, because that would be really cool if it was Rob's song." Cool? That may be the biggest understatement of the century!

Catherine couldn't confirm that Robert's impromptu "Bella's Lullaby" made the final cut. She said to MTV, "'Bella's Lullaby,' actually . . . that's a beautiful love theme that develops and goes all the way through the movie. You see it like in the most beginning parts, and then it gets really into the full song in the middle [of the movie], and then you hear bits of it later. But Rob has two other songs in the movie." When prodded to reveal more about Robert's compositions prior to the movie's release, Catherine demurred, wanting fans to experience it for themselves when they see the movie. What she did reveal was that "they're really beautiful love songs, like heartbreaking. I cried the first time I heard the two songs. They're deep; they're very soulful." Kristen Stewart, the actress who plays

Bella, agrees and confirms Catherine's faith in Robert's music, saying simply, "He plays spontaneously, brilliantly."

Stephenie Meyer never expected the movie casting directors to find a guy who looked so much like the Edward in her mind, so she was doubly delighted that Robert not only looked perfect but was a musician, too. In an early MTV interview about the making of the movie, she was happily surprised by that revelation. "That's something I didn't know," she said. "I've never heard him play, so it's kind of hard to say [whether his lullaby will be as I imagined it]. If it worked out right, it would be really cool." Music has been indispensable to Stephenie's writing process from the start, and for all four books. She explained to the *Los Angeles Times*, "The music is a part of (my writing process). I could not do without it." She elaborated on that process to *Rolling Stone*, saying, "I listen to music always when I write. When I hear music on the radio, I'm like 'Oh! That's a song for this character' or 'This one would so fit that character in this mood!'"

Stephenie's tastes in music are maybe a bit more edgy than Robert's folksy style, though, since she leans toward alternative and progressive metal. Her favorite band *is* British, a trio called Muse, whose song "Time Is Running Out" is part of Stephenie's personal *Twilight* playlist, along with music from bands like Linkin Park and My Chemical Romance. So it's no surprise that Muse is an official part of the movie soundtrack—or that Stephenie's passion for the band was also shared by the moviemakers. Another favorite band of hers, Blue October, fronted by Justin Furstenfeld, played a number of concerts coinciding with the release of *Breaking Dawn*. Stephenie discovered Blue October when she heard the single "Hate Me" in the car one day. She said to *Rolling Stone* that it sounded "like Edward was singing out of my radio."

Though Robert may differ from Stephenie on favorite styles of music, it's obvious that they share a passion for it, and that fact will only serve their collaboration well. Fans in the United Kingdom may be lucky enough to hear some of Robert's musical work in the gigs he and his band play around London, but U.S. fans will have to settle for hearing him perform in *Twilight*. Though Robert did have a MySpace music page under his stage name, Bobby Dupea, he's made the profile private and gone incognito for the time being. Music is still a very personal facet of his life, and he probably isn't quite ready for the multitudes of fans to discover it. For now, anyway. It doesn't seem like too much to hope that with his well-earned time off, he'll finally get around to making the album he's wanted to record for years—and maybe even go on an American tour!

The *Twilight* Phenomenon

"There's something that happens to you when you're first introduced to the phenomenon that is *Twilight* . . . it ignites something inside of you." —*H Magazine*

In 2003, around the same time that Robert Pattinson first met *Goblet of Fire* director Mike Newell, a woman named Stephenie Meyer had a dream. Back then, no one particularly cared what Stephenie Meyer dreamed, or thought, or even wrote, because Stephenie Meyer wasn't a name anyone knew yet—she was a wife and mom living in Arizona. Shocking as it seems now, when there's a world full of extremely loyal and vocal fans who can think of little else, back then, Edward

Cullen, Bella Swan, and Jacob Black existed in only one person's imagination.

Four years later, *Twilight* has sold ten million copies and counting, but as the bestselling author tells it, the novel started on June 2, 2003, with that single dream. Stephenie's dream was about first love, in the most intense possible way. Eventually that dream was transformed into the famous "meadow scene" in the book, in which Bella first sees Edward in his full glittering, vampiric glory, and they profess their love for each other, all the while knowing it could mean a tragic end. This swoon-worthy moment was one of the most anticipated movie scenes for fans, who hoped that Robert Pattinson and Kristen Stewart's chemistry would match the power of the scene they have imagined in their own minds, as they read (and reread) the novel. Luckily Stephenie has a well-trafficked website where she could assure her Twilighters that it would. After a visit to the set, she crowed that *Twilight* devotees were going to get all they hoped for and more. Gleeful, she wrote, "They are amazing actors. . . . They are channeling Edward and Bella like nobody's business."

Let's get back to that spicy dream. How—exactly—did that climactic moment between Edward and Bella begin? We can all be thankful that Stephenie woke with it still in her mind in such vivid detail. As she remembers it, a strikingly beautiful vampire boy and an ordinary teenage girl stood in a sunny meadow, talking about their extraordinary connection. Something was compelling them to be together . . . and yet how could that be? They were doomed because of one unavoidable truth: Every second they were together, the vampire was longing to kill the girl. And then Stephenie woke up.

Like anyone waking up in the middle of a great dream before she wanted to, Stephenie was *Not. Pleased. At. All.* She wanted to know more, to keep eavesdropping on this fascinating and beautiful couple—and she couldn't stop thinking about what might have happened for the star-crossed teens. She ended up not mentioning it to her husband, and she knew that she couldn't just call her friends or siblings and tell them about the dream. As she later said to CBS News, "Everybody *hates* that!" Still, she continued to wonder—constantly—about what might happen next for the oddly matched couple in her dream.

So in between the tasks of her day—making lunch, taking her three small sons, then ages one, three, and five, to swimming lessons—Stephenie decided to try capturing the dream on paper. She began to write the rest of the scene as she imagined it, conjuring as much of the moody atmosphere as she could. She wrote ten pages that day, but felt like she wasn't typing fast enough to keep up with what was happening as the story unfolded inside her head. Somehow, she'd managed to tap back into the force that had created the dream in the first place, but harnessing it was another matter. So she wrote again the next day, and the next, and soon she had moved a desk into the middle of her living room so that she could write while watching her children play.

Stephenie had earned her English degree from Brigham Young University in 1995, so she was no stranger to writing. But this was unlike any writing experience she'd ever had before. The story positively flowed from her fingertips, in a way that her college English papers had never seemed to do. Stephenie could hear the couple's voices clearly in her head. All she had to do was keep up with their conversations. She got the bulk of her writing done late at night, while her family slept, music blasting through her headphones—music that she would soon come to think of as the soundtrack for her story. She realized that music was an integral part of story writing for her. In the years since *Twilight*'s publication, Stephenie has published playlists for each of the four books in the Twilight Saga on her website, explaining to fans that the songs inspired her while writing. Sometimes they have even suggested plotlines or character development. As she explained to *Rolling Stone*, several years after the totally unexpected first blaze of writing that became *Twilight*, and even after the books had become an explosive success, "I really don't think you get a dream like that more than once in your lifetime. And I didn't need it; once I had the story and it unlocked the writer inside me, I had enough ideas on my own."

As she wrote, Stephenie got up the courage to tell her older sister, Emily, about the book and eventually let her read along, chapter by chapter, as it flowed out of her. Emily is an avid *Buffy the Vampire Slayer* fan, so of course she suggested that Stephenie borrow the *Buffy* DVDs to see another take on how the vampire myths and legends could exist in a modern high school setting. But Stephenie was adamant about not wanting other influences in her head as she wrote. Interviewers are often shocked to discover that for an author of vampire stories, Stephenie is surprisingly unfamiliar with the canon of vampire books and movies. Fans of the Twilight Saga should be relieved that Stephenie played the role of stubborn little sister and *didn't* listen to Emily's advice. The end result was that Stephenie created the original world of *Twilight* and its dazzlingly different vampire citizens all from her own vivid imagination.

Stephenie's vampires aren't your typical vampires. They're vampire "vegetarians"—they don't allow themselves to enjoy human prey. They abstain from drinking human blood, and instead they hunt animals, from mountain lions to elk to grizzlies, and drink *their* blood. As Stephenie explains to fans on her MySpace profile, "It's like living on a diet forever, no cheating. Sigh." A hard limitation to set on yourself, but it's a sacrifice that her vampires—the good ones, at least— have decided they are willing to make.

With the Cullen family—the coven of vampires who are the pseudo-family to which Edward belongs— Stephenie was proud that she'd invented a whole new kind of mythology for the vampires that lived in her world. These were not vampires who could only come out at night, or ones who were hunted down with crosses and garlic. Not at all! Her vampires are, essentially, made from living stone. They are incredibly strong, amazingly fast, and perfectly gorgeous creatures. They stay out of the sun not because it burns them, but because they have a tendency to sparkle in it. The stonelike substance that makes up their bodies holds facets of light, just like diamonds. Basically they are enhanced in every way possible from the humans they once were before becoming vampires. Oh, and they can only be killed by being torn apart from limb to limb, and then burned (easy, right?). All of these details, and their accuracy within the *Twilight* universe, matter enormously to Stephenie and her fans. That's why much later, when it came time to sell movie rights, Stephenie had to go to someone who would honor what she had created and her fans loved. It was director Catherine Hardwicke's similar vision—that and her promise of "No garlic, no crosses, no fangs!"—that won Stephenie's trust that she was giving her imagined world to the right person, the one who could bring it to cinematic life.

Stephenie *was* thinking about a movie, even as she wrote the first draft of *Twilight*. Not that she believed the book would even get published when she was first starting—*that* would have been crazy, a chance in a zillion! But it was *fun* casting the actors in her head. She explained to fans later on premiere.com, "I saw the book very visually as I was writing it," so picturing a movie was a natural extension. "Just to see one scene of it on the big screen [would be worth it]," she went on. "I didn't care about anyone else going to see it. This was about me, alone, in the theater getting to see it on the screen and having it be real, and that's what swayed me [to take the risk allowing it to become Catherine Hardwicke's movie]."

But let's get back to how *Twilight* ever got into the hands of its very first fan to begin with. Stephenie had that pivotal dream at the beginning of June, and by the end of August, she had a completed novel manuscript in her hands. That's none too shabby for the equivalent of a summer vacation! Once she had that finished piece of writing, she began to send the manuscript out to literary agents, with the stand-in title, *Forks,* after the town in Washington State that serves as the setting for much of the story's action. It was then that things started to happen for Stephenie, and happen with a speed that first-time authors rarely experience. But then again, she had already known that this story wasn't like any other. She crossed her fingers, hoping that other people would recognize that, too.

Inevitably, they did. Jodi Reamer, an agent with Writers House, a highly regarded New York literary agency, called soon after reading the manuscript, asking to represent Stephenie and her novel. In one of the first significant decisions about the book, before sending the manuscript out to editors, Jodi suggested that she and Stephenie try to find a new title "with more atmosphere." They brainstormed for a week, and the result was *Twilight*—evocative, sweeping, lush, and now familiar to millions of readers. Interestingly enough, though, there simply may not be a perfect title for this book, Stephenie says on her website. When the book began to be published in different countries, hardly any stuck with the title *Twilight*. In Germany, the book is called *Until Dawn*, but in German it sounds like *until bite*, so the German title is a vampire pun. In Finland, the title is *Temptation*, and in France, *Fascination*. The Japanese publisher split *Twilight* into three separate books: *The Boy I Love Is a Vampire*, *Blood Tastes Sadness*, and *The Vampire Family in the Darkness*.

Once Stephenie had the perfect title (at least for America), off the manuscript went to publishing houses. Then, with vampirelike speed, Stephenie had an editor. Megan Tingley, of Little, Brown Books for Young Readers, was so taken by Stephenie's vision that she decided she wanted to publish not just *Twilight*, but two more books, which Stephenie hadn't even written yet.

Twilight was published on October 5, 2005, and almost instantly, readers embraced it. Why? Well, for a million reasons, many of them Edward, Edward, and . . . Edward! But one of the other reasons is the very one that Robert Pattinson himself mentioned to MTV: "It's very intimate. . . . At the core of *Twilight*, it's a love story. It's a very intense love story, which differentiates it. Everything else just goes away."

Not only did readers embrace and love the book, they wanted to *talk* about it. They wanted to talk about Bella, about Edward, about romance, and choices, and the perfect guy, and all the oh-so-sexy moments between these characters that feel incredibly *real*. So *Twilight* fans flocked to the Internet. Many of them had done the same a few years earlier, when they read and loved the Harry Potter books and wanted to find other people who did, too. Within a month of *Twilight*'s release, fan sites began popping up. And those early fan sites were lucky beyond their wildest dreams—they often got drop-in visits from Stephenie Meyer herself. Stephenie was just as eager to talk to her readers as they were to talk to her. She read their fan fiction, answered questions about the mythology of her vampire world, and was genuinely awed by the fervor of the teens who loved her story. Stephenie had never actually heard of MySpace before she began visiting *Twilight* fan sites, but once the Twihards told her about it, she signed up. Today she has more than 75,000 MySpace friends! Her Top 25 includes her absolute favorite band, Muse; actor Henry Cavill, who Stephenie once hoped would play the role of Edward; her publicist, Elizabeth; and her younger brother, Jacob (!), to name a few. She also helped establish some of the fan sites in those early days. She supported Lori Joffs, a Nashville stay-at-home mom who founded The Twilight Lexicon (www.twilightlexicon. com), by providing backstories and other intriguing details about the characters and the world of *Twilight* that couldn't be found anywhere else at the time.

For the next three years, each end of summer meant not just that school was about to start, but that Stephenie had published a new addition to what became known as the Twilight Saga. As each one hit the bookstores, the clamor and love for the books grew and grew, with markers such as the *New York Times* bestsellerdom for every volume, thousands upon thousands of book preorders by eager fans, and sold-out "Twilight Proms." Some of the proms had the luck to host Stephenie herself, like the five-hundred-guest sold-out event on May 5, 2007, at Arizona State University, where Stephenie got into the prom spirit herself, arriving in a gorgeous burgundy gown with her dark hair curled in ringlets.

Twilight had become a phenomenon! With that came growing anticipation about the issue at the heart of the stories: Who would Bella Swan choose to devote herself to? Would it be her faithful but absent vampire love, Edward? Or dependable, lovable Jacob Black, the werewolf who is always there when she needs him? Before long, readers began pro-claiming their loyalty for one suitor over the other in public places, wearing customized shirts—and even shoes!—emblazoned with the words TEAM JACOB or TEAM EDWARD. They started even more fan sites, along with MySpace and Facebook groups to discuss the many reasons why they felt that Bella would eventually see things their way.

Most of all, though, readers simply talked about the books. They gulped down each new book, usually in one frenzied night of must-know-the-ending reading, and then passed it to their friends, sisters, cousins, and boyfriends. Obviously some girls have better luck than others in getting their boyfriends to read it. But it's not just people their own ages that *Twilight* fans share the book with. They also share it with their moms, who have become just as besotted as their daughters. In fact, one of the most active online fan sites is called Twilight Moms (www.twilightmoms.com), which labels itself a home for fans of Stephenie Meyer

Robert Pattinson:
From Schoolboy to Star

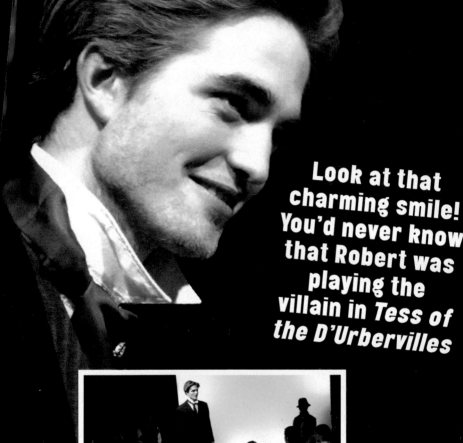

Look at that charming smile! You'd never know that Robert was playing the villain in *Tess of the D'Urbervilles*

Robert commands onstage attention from his fellow actors in one of his earliest roles.

Robert steals a kiss from his castmate . . .

walks the red carpet with his first big-screen sweetheart, Katie Leung . . .

and slips into character with his Bella co-star Kristen Stewart.

Even in a T-shirt, Rob can steal your heart. . . .

And look at those dreamy eyes and chiseled cheekbones!

Robert perfects the
brooding stare that
his fans adore.

Robert flashes the dazzling smile that could win any girl's heart.

Robert studies last-minute line changes before stepping in front of the cameras.

While filming *Twilight* on-set in Kalama, Washington, Robert makes an escape from watching eyes.

Robert pauses to get into character before filming a scene from *Twilight*.

**Who can resist Edward Cullen...
or Robert Pattinson?**

to "become friends while balancing family, work, AND our *Twilight* addiction." At the cast's first public appearance in San Diego, at a convention called Comic-Con, it was a *Twilight* Mom who got up to the microphone to ask Robert Pattinson and his co-star Taylor Lautner, who plays Jacob, one of the most daring questions they've ever been asked in public, "So guys, is it boxers, briefs, or nothing?" Wow! We'll never know whether Robert and Taylor answered the question, or artfully dodged it, since the six thousand fans filling the auditorium went wild, and all that could be heard were their thrilled screams.

According to hollywoodreporter.com, so many fans flooded toward the *Twilight* booth at Comic-Con that the fire marshal had to shut down the area for part of the afternoon. That must have caused some very loud screaming! Many of those fans had camped out overnight for "a chance to see early footage of the film and get a glimpse at the cast of heartthrobs set to bring the teen-vampire tale to life," CNN reported.

Variety newspaper blogger Anne Thompson went so far as to name Robert as the number one hunk of Comic-Con! And for the uninitiated still asking, "Why all the fuss over a book series?" one fan, eighteen-year-old Emma Quan, gave a perfect answer to CNN, "It's a really good love story that has fantasy. It's like *Harry Potter* plus romance plus good-looking people." No doubt similar Q&A's will keep happening all across the world until there are few people left who can claim that they've never heard of *Twilight*.

How else has *Twilight* changed our world? Well, obviously, it's an inspiration, as tales of love often are. There are thousands of pieces of fan fiction online, along with fan art, not to mention all those TEAM EDWARD and TEAM JACOB shirts. And *Twilight* director Catherine Hardwicke and author Stephenie Meyer find fans' projects to be tremendously inspiring. Catherine told bloodydisgusting.com, "It's cool that it's so creative for people, they are making their own trailers and songs and it has sparked a creative explosion. I think it's really exciting." The Twilight Saga has sparked music, too! The Bella Cullen Project is the most well-known. The band is made up of a group of three friends who started playing *Twilight*-inspired music while in high school, and who have produced a CD of *Twilight*-themed songs, including titles like "VampWolf," "Sexy Vampire," and "Switzerland." It's not all just girl bands, though. The Mitch Hansen Band from Atlanta, Georgia, has been strongly affected by Stephenie's work, too. The band has a CD called *The Twilight Hour*, with songs titled "Lullaby" and "Jacob Black." Both bands are sure to play sold-out shows to *Twilight* fans in their local areas—and across the country if they choose to go on tour. Who doesn't want to hear resonant songs about the deep and abiding love Bella and Edward have, or the angsty conflict of her impending choice between vampire and werewolf, or mortal and immortal life?

It's rich material to mine for the aching songs that touch music listeners. As we know, Robert Pattinson felt the pull to create music out of this tragic love story. Along with all the music and T-shirts and buttons, countless blogs have sprung up about *Twilight* love, including one called *Twilight* Guy (www. twilightguy.com), in which a nineteen-year-old guy blogs about his research into the minds of *Twilight* lovers. Or as he puts it, "I am trying to find why nearly every girl in the world is obsessed with the *Twilight* books by Stephenie Meyer!"

So what does one call a fan of *Twilight*, anyway? As with all things related to the books (and the movie), there are strongly held, differing opinions. Two nicknames seem to be the most common. One of the first nicknames was the most obvious: Twilighters, which has a nice ring to it. The other is Twihards, a title that was coined by *Twilight* actor Michael Welch, who plays the role of Mike Newton, Bella's ardent (but boringly human) admirer. Michael first used the term on his blog (www.michaelwelchonline.com), directed fondly at the fans who had already expressed so much interest in his new movie role. *Twilight* has invaded the way we speak beyond the invention of names for fans, though. If you haven't heard someone use the term "OME" (Oh My Edward) or "OMJ" (Oh My Jacob), you've probably been asleep for, like, the last year. But whatever expressions you use, or whatever you call yourself—Twilighter, Twihard, Fanpire, or just a charter member of a "Who cares what we're called, what matters is that Edward is so hot!" group on Facebook or MySpace—what really matters is sharing that love with other fans who feel just the same way you do about all things *Twilight* related.

And that's what the hype is all about—being one of the many fans. It's how we are connecting and sharing our passion for these characters and their story with millions of other *Twilight* lovers. "The story is just so intimate that people really think they know the characters and can feel the emotions and stuff so people attach themselves to it," Robert said to MTV about the pull of Bella and Edward's story. Of course, as with anything that's incredibly popular, there are skeptics and disbelievers. But for anyone who doesn't quite believe that the *Twilight* phenomenon is, well, a phenomenon, go to eBay and try buying one of the rare, prepublication, unfinished editions of *Twilight* that was created for book reviewers and other key players in the entertainment industry. When these advanced readers copies (ARCs) do appear, they typically sell for hundreds of dollars—and even more if they're signed by Stephenie.

The phenomenon only grew bigger once the movie of *Twilight* was announced. Fans had been waiting for their movie for a long time, and blogging about who they'd cast as Bella and Edward, or what songs just *had* to be on the soundtrack. When the news finally broke, they went nuts—in the best, most enthusiastic way! In fact, there were more than fifty thousand posts on IMDb.com within the first forty-eight hours after the movie was announced. And when the trailer for *Twilight* went up, as Bella would say, "Holy crow!"

Fans rapidly made it the most-watched movie trailer of all time—it had even more views than the new Indiana Jones movie. For those of us who have been fans of the Twilight Saga since the beginning, it is amazing to ponder how quickly its popularity has increased. But since we know how impossible it is to resist sharing something we love so much, the widespread reach of *Twilight* isn't all surprising. And it all comes down to one really simple fact, one that Catherine Hardwicke shared in an interview with IGN.com: "The book has a heart and soul that makes everybody love it."

Oh My Edward!

7

"I never anticipated that Rob would end up looking like the actor in my head. When he's Rob, he's just Rob, and he's funny . . . and then, at the snap of a finger, he just switches into Edward, and it's kind of an amazing transformation to watch." —*Stephenie Meyer*

At San Diego's Comic-Con in July 2008, Rob was asked what attracted him to the role, but there was so much screaming he said he couldn't concentrate. Try as he might to be a Serious Actor, and come up with a distinguished, thoughtful, meaningful answer, all the adoring attention was just too much for this shy sweetheart. So he gave up. What else could he do? With a bashful, but tickled smile, he said, "I just wanted to play the hottest vampire in the world. It hurts me to think of myself." Not only can this cutie play a century-old vampire with startling intensity, but he can look at the astonishing attention being heaped on him with a level head and tongue-in-cheek wit.

How *did* Robert Thomas-Pattinson get chosen for the sacred role of Edward Anthony Masen Cullen? Well, to say that the auditions were competitive is putting it mildly. More than five thousand professional actors auditioned for the role! Let's back up for just a second, though, to see how the role of Edward in a movie version of *Twilight* even came into existence. Not terribly long after *Twilight* was published, Stephenie Meyer sold the rights to produce the movie to Paramount's MTV films. Much to her dismay, the script they developed for the movie was completely unlike the books. In fact, as Stephenie later told *Entertainment Weekly* interviewers, "They could have put that movie out, called it something

else, and no one would have known it was *Twilight*."
Stephenie couldn't let that happen, since she knew
her loyal Twilighters would never stand for it. So after
Paramount's option expired, Stephenie was nervous
about letting anyone even *think* about producing a
movie of one of her books again. But then Eric Feig,
president of production at Summit Entertainment, set
out on a mission to change her mind. Eventually he
convinced a hesitant Stephenie that his vision for a
movie matched hers. The clincher was a guarantee he
made to her. The contract his company signed with
her included a promise that "no vampire character
will be depicted with canine or incisor teeth longer
or more pronounced than may be found in human
beings," and other key non-negotiable points that Stephenie insisted on for the integrity of her books—and
that Summit happily agreed to. And so, in July 2007,
Stephenie and Summit Entertainment announced that
Twilight would be going into production.

Instantly fans began to theorize for hours on end

about which actors might fill the roles. They knew from reading Stephenie's website and from various interviews and chats with her on fan sites that she had someone in particular marked as her first choice. She knew that authors didn't usually get any say in the casting of a movie, even if it was one based on their work, but she would have given the part of Edward to Henry Cavill. But this was when he was barely in his twenties, somewhere back in the time when Paramount was writing scripts for their never-produced version of *Twilight*. As Stephenie reluctantly but cheerfully later explained on her website, "Meanwhile, years have passed, my actors have aged, and I think the time has come to recast the *Twilight* movie. (For fun, of course! I still have no say in who gets hired.) The most disappointing thing for me is losing my perfect Edward. Henry Cavill is now twenty-four years old. Let us have a moment of quiet in which to mourn. . . ."

While Stephenie's fans were filling up message

boards full of new casting suggestions, director Catherine Hardwicke was busy overseeing the writing of the screenplay. Because of an impending screenwriters' strike, it had to be finished in six weeks! She was also thinking about aspects like where to film, how to make vampire skin sparkle like diamonds, oh, and yeah, who her lead actors should be. It was clear from the start that Catherine felt strongly about the story itself—as she explained to *Entertainment Weekly,* "When I read the book, I could almost feel Bella breathing." Her enthusiasm has only grown since. As she gushed to bloodydisgusting.com, "I love this world. I fell in love with Stephenie's world the first time I read it, it's like I'm there! I want to see it, I want to breathe it in and see it come to life." She was committed to the idea that Bella should be played by an actual teen in order to convey all of Bella's teen emotions as realistically as possible. But holding the lead role in a movie is no small task, even for seasoned pros, much less for a young teen actress.

Casting Kristen Stewart in the role of Bella actually turned out to be surprisingly uncomplicated, though. As she told *Entertainment Weekly*, Catherine Hardwicke had seen Kristen in Sean Penn's *Into the Wild* the previous year. "Her mixture of innocence and longing just knocked me out," Catherine says. That performance of Kristen's stayed with Catherine, and she knew she wanted Kristen as her Bella. Hoping to make it happen, she sent the script to Kristen, and then took a red-eye flight from LA to Pittsburgh. The seventeen-year-old actress was there filming another movie, *Adventureland*, and Catherine wanted to do an impromptu screen test with her. "She'd been shooting all night, but she learned her lines on the spot," Catherine remembers. "She danced on the bed and chased pigeons in the park. I was captivated." As Kristen tells it, although she hadn't read the books, once that script arrived in Pittsburgh, she knew it was a part she wanted. When *TV Guide* asked her what made her decide to take the part, she answered without any hesitation, "The love story. I know it's really simple and really basic, but I think that's what pushes humans to go to crazy limits—love. If somebody ever dies for somebody, it's because they love them. And for me, this was the most epic love story, and I wanted to give it a shot."

With her Bella secured, Catherine turned her attention to the challenging job of finding an actor who could pull off the part of being the world's hottest vampire. "Everybody has such an idealized vision of Edward," she told *Entertainment Weekly*. "They [the book's fans] were rabid. Like, old ladies saying, 'You better get it right.'" Well, maybe not like old ladies. But of course fans wanted the movie's Edward to look like . . . *Edward.* Twilighters hold him as close to their hearts as Bella does. He's dazzling, literally and figuratively. Edward is a century-old vampire who will be seventeen eternally. Unfailingly polite, unbelievably self-controlled and moral, dedicated and protective almost beyond reason—and with the perfect face of an angel. To Bella, there is nothing in the world better than Edward. How could any mere mortal actor live up to that image?

Initially Catherine wasn't sure that Robert Pattinson matched even *her* image of Edward. But Rob won her over. How? He flew to meet Catherine at her home in Venice, California, where she promptly threw him into a love scene with Kristen as an audition. A love scene on—*ahem*—Catherine's bed! In a cover story with *Entertainment Weekly*, Catherine described the moments that followed as "electric." "The room shorted out, the sky opened up, and I was like, 'This is going to be good.'" The chemistry convinced Catherine that Rob and no one but Rob could be Edward. On December 11, 2007, Summit Entertainment announced that Robert Pattinson would be starring opposite Kristen Stewart. Stephenie Meyer announced the news on her blog, too, practically *squee*-ing like one of her own fan girls. Absolutely delighted, she informed her readers, "I am ecstatic with Summit's choice for

Edward. There are very few actors who can look both dangerous and beautiful at the same time, and even fewer who I can picture in my head as Edward. Robert Pattinson is going to be amazing."

At first, though, not everyone agreed. If it seemed there had been lots of online buzz and chatter and debate *before* the role of Edward was cast, that was nothing compared to the intense reactions of fans afterward. On one side were the girls who looked at Rob and saw only Edward, just as they pictured him. On the other were the ones vehemently insisting that he seemed nothing—nothing!—like the Edward in their dreams. While Robert can (mostly) laugh about it now, he admits that the swift and definitively negative response of angry, anti-Rob fans caught him off guard. In part, this was because he'd grown used to the existence of online fan forums being helpful. In an interview after the opening of *Goblet of Fire*, he admitted to mymovies.net, "I read a lot online [on the fan sites] and the comments were really helpful." Fans' comments aided him in catching the little details and nuances of being Cedric that he'd completely overlooked, even after poring over the book, and helped him confirm that playing Cedric as "the strong, silent type" was the way to go.

So Rob was taken aback by the intensely negative reaction some fans had when they learned he was playing the coveted role of Edward. He explained to the L.A. Times that it was his mom who noticed first. "There was this torrent of abuse at the beginning that my mum made me aware of—she sent me this link to this petition that said, 'Please! Anyone else apart from him!'" Ouch, Mrs. Pattinson! It looks like even fine celebrities have to put up with mildly annoying parentals. Much of the fans' debate online had to do with re-envisioning the actor who played Cedric as anyone other than, well, Cedric, but even more, it had to do with a very blunt question. Was Rob hot enough to be Edward, or would he do an injustice to Stephenie Meyer's vision of a perfectly created vampire god? Fellow cast member Michael Welch says it best. Michael plays poor Mike Newton, who has a crush on Bella and doesn't stand a chance against the charms of Edward. He was one of the five thousand other actors who initially auditioned for the role of Edward, but in an interview with mania.com, he laid out his good-natured opinion: "Let's face it, this movie lives and dies on that boy's chiseled face and I'm glad it's him to carry that weight and not me."

Thankfully Rob was able to channel the criticisms in a way that ultimately helped him understand his character even more thoroughly. As he explained to MSN.com, "I thought I couldn't deal with the humiliation of 'Could he be more good looking?' Then I kind of read it [as] it's not like the author is saying Edward *is* the best-looking guy in the world; it's from Bella's perspective who is obsessed with him. When you take into account that, he could look like anything. When you are in love with someone, you look past all the flaws." And he laughingly elaborated on this understanding of his character and Bella's fanatical adoration to teenhollywood.com, saying, "He could be a piece of cheese and she'd say the same thing." From the point he realized that, Rob started looking ahead, determined to prove to the fans that he could, in fact, embody Edward like no other actor could.

Robert Pattinson truly understood the concerns of the book's fans because he shares in the passion for the novels himself. He came a little late to the Twilight Saga—but Taylor Lautner, who was cast as Jacob Black, was a fan before he landed the role. Taylor won big points for Team Jacob by revealing that a friend had introduced him to the books long before he auditioned for the role. He told reelzchannel.com that after reading them, "I understand their passion for the book because I'm just as passionate for it. . . . I'm just like any of those crazy girl fans out there," when it comes to enthusiasm for the book series. But Rob shot back, "Once I'd read the first book, I knew that, whether or not I got cast, I was going to read the other books. Definitely," in an interview with teenhollywood.com, which helped him to win back the hearts of Twilighters.

In fact, Robert initially shared the Twihards' worry. After reading the book, he was totally unnerved by the descriptions of Edward as "perfect" and "gorgeous." As he reminisced to teenhollywood.com, "After the casting people talked to me and said, 'Read the book.' I did and I just thought, 'This is really dumb. It's just so pointless for me, even going up for it.'" Nearly two years later, we're certainly glad that he didn't decide to write off the idea of auditioning! Of course, Robert's attention to the concerns of his fans goes deeper than sparkly skin-deep. As he explained in an interview to G4.com, a gaming and entertainment website, "It's intimidating because you're stepping into somebody's imagination, which doesn't always happen. When a movie comes out and there's no book first, then they sit down and you sort of have an offering and they sit down with more open minds. Here, they have a slot and they want you to fill it. That can be quite intimidating."

Throwing himself into his role—in spite of, or *because* of, the concerns of the fans—was a task that Robert took very seriously. Remember, this is a guy who is ready to prove to the world he's a serious young actor with a long and worthy career before him. So he traveled to Washington State ahead of the rest of the cast. He wanted to spend time in solitude, getting to know himself as the character of Edward. What's his method for finding a deep understanding of a character? Well, in this case, he wrote journal entries as Edward, and separated himself from his friends and family. "I wanted to feel his isolation," he told *Entertainment Weekly*. Still, Rob didn't force himself to embody Edward in *every way*. "I was supposed to get a six-pack," he quips, "but it didn't really work out." (Get the pun . . . "work out"?) And he didn't test out Edward's cravings by hunting down the wildlife in Washington and drinking their blood . . .

well, at least, not that we know about! Catherine Hardwicke isn't so sure, though, as she whispered to Andrew Sim of darkhorizons.com during his set visit, "In fact, I hate to say this, but there's a couple girls in Portland . . . he bit their necks and drank their blood— two days ago at a bar." Very funny, Catherine, but we're sure that Rob was hardly menacing the girls in Portland, unless he was just making them swoon as usual—and that's not really a menace!

The time spent alone and thinking helped Robert get inside the head of Edward and shape him into the character that moviegoers will see played out on the big screen. "I had to formulate my own idea of who the guy is anyway. I mean, it's a little bit more pressure, but there's no point in acknowledging what other people think about it. The only thing you can do is try to find some element of truth to yourself." What are the "elements of truth" to Edward that Robert found? Well, mostly it's that, in actuality, Edward is far from the godlike perfection that Bella—and the members of

Team Edward—imagine him to be. As he elaborated for MTV.com, "He's supposed to be the perfect guy but that's from Bella's perspective, who's completely, madly in love with him. She's tremendously obsessed with him. So you can never take anything to be a fact. It's just her opinion of him. And he seems to hate himself and everything about him. So you've got to have the compromise between the two to figure out who he is as much as possible because there are very few actual facts about him."

Really? An Edward who is full of doubt and self-loathing, instead of one who is the proudest, strongest, hottest undead being in existence? Could Robert have it all wrong? Well, it's a mind shift, all right. Before you get too far down the road of wondering if Rob has lost his mind, or is thinking of an altogether different character from the one we know and love, you should know that there's one Very Important Person who pretty much agrees with him . . . she sees Edward the same way. Author Stephenie Meyer gave Robert an important—and exclusive—look at a project that would help Robert really understand his character. She showed him the not-yet-completed manuscript she's writing called *Midnight Sun*.

Midnight Sun lays out the events of *Twilight* all over again, but this time from Edward's perspective. After reading it, Robert was relieved, he told MSN.com, because in Stephenie's understanding, Edward "just sees himself as the most disgusting person in the entire world, which is how I was trying to play it before I read that. Luckily, I was on the same page as the author." In another interview, this one with the *L.A. Times*, he elaborated on what he learned from Stephenie's unpublished Edward-centric version of *Twilight*. "In *Midnight Sun*, you find that he hides a lot from her, you find out the things that he's hidden. Even basic things like there are other vampires who are going to kill her; I mean he kind of lies about it for ages." And he went on to explain why this makes sense, "It was kind of a deceptively complicated character to play.

When you look at what Edward says, it seems like he always says the right thing. Always just the perfect gentleman. But when you put it in the context of his actual life situation and it doesn't compute that he would be this completely easygoing, normal guy. That's what he was before [when he was human], then he got bit [and turned into a vampire]. He's still trying to be a nice guy, but he's also now killed like fifty people, so he's kind of in a state of constant penance."

So how *would* Robert define Edward? Well, it's kinda heartbreakingly sentimental, really. "He's a guy who's just incredibly frustrated and he finds this one thing which is his and he can't keep it safe, and that's almost impossible for him to handle." Aww. Somehow, that thought just makes us love Rob—and Edward—all the more.

Lights, Camera, *Twilight*!

**"They just caught the essence of it.
Edward and Bella have just that same
feeling as they do in the book."**
—Stephenie Meyer

Everyone has a favorite Edward and Bella moment.
The one you feel completely embodies the epic, tragic
romanticism of their relationship, the one you've most
awaited seeing on the big screen in all its glorious
perfection. And Robert Pattinson in all *his* glorious
perfection. At San Diego's Comic-Con, Catherine
Hardwicke and Stephenie Meyer revealed that they
have their own favorite Edward and Bella moments,
too. Stephenie's favorite moment from the film version

of *Twilight* is the scene in the hospital after Edward saves Bella from nearly being killed in a car accident in the high school parking lot. Bella is trying to confront Edward about what happened, and get him to tell her the truth. Stephenie thinks the scene crackles with tension between Kristen and Robert, capturing the moment just as she'd envisioned it. Catherine's choice is another scene in which Bella forces the truth from Edward, this time after the fateful trip to Port Angeles, when Edward must come to Bella's aid. Bella presses Edward to admit that he's a vampire, asking him how old he is, and when he replies, "Seventeen," she pushes harder, demanding, "How long have you been seventeen?"

Stephenie and Catherine aren't the only ones with favorite on-screen moments—Robert and Kristen have theirs as well. Robert, ever humble, and committed to Edward's vision of himself as not good enough for Bella, admits that his favorite scene wasn't one of the flashy, action-packed vampire scenes, or one when Bella's professing her love for him. No, the Bella-Edward moment closest to Robert's heart is one where Bella's cutting Edward down to size. "My favorite scene was a little scene with Kristen where I'm trying to intimidate her and then she doesn't get intimidated and she's not scared of me. At all," he said with a big smile during the Comic-Con panel. He was thrilled to realize that he and Stephenie were talking about the same scene—talk about a real connection between the author and her character-come-to-life!

Kristen didn't want to be held to just one of Bella's scenes, so she gave the screaming fans two favorites. "There's a part where we have to leave each other," she said. "It's a sweet moment, but it's really sad. She's going off with Alice down to Phoenix and it's the first time that they've actually had to say good-bye to each other. Bella's worried that they're not ever going to see each other again. That was good." That heartbreaking scene is near the end of the story, but there's another that is exclusive to the movie—it came entirely out of an afternoon of improvisation during the famous meadow scene. "We were frolicking in the leaves and laying around, and she's being cocky," Kristen said, "and I stick my finger in his mouth and say, 'Want a taste?'" Wow! Steamy! Kristen couldn't guarantee that the scene would make it into the movie's final cut, but she hopes that it does. And now, so do Twihards everywhere, who didn't think that meadow scene could get any better than it already was in the novel.

What's clear from all these descriptions added up is that Robert and Kristen have brought fresh new insights and depth into already-beloved characters. That's what makes these two boilin'-hot stars ones to watch out for *and* it's what makes *Twilight* one of the most anticipated movies of 2008. "It's like Romeo and Juliet . . . you can't let anybody else know what's going on, but you are compelled . . . you have to see where it goes. Period," Kristen Stewart said. Peter Facinelli, who plays Dr. Cullen, has a similar—if slightly less romantic—perception of the story, though. "It's *Romeo and Juliet* squared. They cannot be together. . . . Plus he has to fight every instinct he has not to eat the girl!"

Filming *Twilight* wasn't always just giddy scenes in the leaves, however. As Robert knew from filming the large-scale *Harry Potter and the Goblet of Fire*, a major Hollywood movie takes a lot of time, work, and patience to create. But the love story of Bella and Edward captured Robert and the rest of the production team. Kristen remarked, "The cool thing about the story is that it's a seemingly wonderful fantasy—let's fall in love with vampires and live forever—but it's so much harder than that. Imagine living forever. Living one life is hard enough." Legions of *Twilight* fans across the world would agree, because they know the amazing experience of reading the books—being completely swept away by the saga, but simultaneously thrilled and terrified at the choice that Bella will eventually have to make. Rob has a similar understanding of why the story is so compelling, one that reveals how deeply he's come to understand the character of Edward. As he told joblo.com, "I mean Edward was so stale for eighty years. He was just . . . all he wanted to do was either die or become human again. When this girl comes, and he kind of . . . it kind of reawakens senses that haven't been around for ages . . . it's basically everything he wants, it's just so fleeting." Whoa.

Catherine agrees with both her actors, explaining that she was drawn to the movie because of the sentiments and themes that she and the actors would get to explore. "How it feels to be in your first love and loving somebody so much that you would literally turn to a vampire. That's pretty cool. That's intense. And that's how we felt most of the time when we're young, or even now. Like 'Oh my God, I would do anything to be with this person.'" It's clear, then, that this really is the ultimate team to create the film version of Twilight, since they all understand the books at the same deep level as the book's true fans.

Being able to share ideas about the story and the conflict that their characters face allowed Robert and Kristen to bond on a level that only added to their chemistry while filming Edward and Bella. MTV interviewers observed, "No one bothers Stewart between takes as she comes back from whatever place she has to go to find her sorrow. On almost every occasion, it is Pattinson who will eventually walk over, give her shoulder a light rub, and bring her back for the next take."

Both Kristen and Robert have agreed that working with each other was a main draw of acting in *Twilight* in the first place. "Kristen's the best actress in this generation and that's why I wanted to do this movie," Robert told MTV. In another interview, with G4.com, he spoke about their goals for their work, saying, "I hope that what Kristen and I have been doing is making it a lot more serious than your average kind of teen [movie]. Even though it's [about] a vampire, it is essentially a teen romance. But I've been trying to get more of the serious aspects." Both Kristen and Robert have such abiding respect for each other's talent and dedication that they can't imagine putting themselves in these vulnerable scenes with anyone else.

At Comic-Con, Kristen said, "It's like the ideal version of love. As a lame sort of sappy girl, that's sort of what life is about." As expected the crowd gave an audible "Awwwwww"—and then went into a frenzied scream as she continued, "Plus, I got to do this audition with Rob Pattinson. It was on Catherine's bed." More screams. "In her bed," Robert teased. "With Catherine." And Kristen can't say enough about how generous Robert is. "He's so good and he's so soulful and he's just not a liar—you can feel pain from him," she said in one interview.

An intern on the *Twilight* set who blogs at imstillwandering.blogspot.com observed an intimate moment between Robert, Kristen, and Catherine as they shot take after take of one Edward-and-Bella scene. She writes, "At one point Rob said, 'I felt like I was falling apart during that take. . . .' and Catherine told him, 'Then go with it. Fall apart. Fall into her. You are falling so into her, just use that.' And of course the following take was flawless." Robert's ability to let go and fall apart is a rare and valuable skill, and one that seems to hint that this young actor is clearly poised to become one of the next great leading men. He puts not only vulnerability into his performance, but passion, too . . . even if sometimes, it's too much passion! When Catherine was asked during the Comic-Con panel whether there were any spontaneous moments on the set worth recounting, she responded, "I've got one! In one of the kissing scenes, Rob got a little passionate and fell off the bed onto the floor." To no one's surprise, the crowd went wild, as Rob blushed and sheepishly grinned out at the screaming audience. Cold and hot, sensitive and fierce, Robert clearly *became* Edward in every possible way.

He did have the benefit of being one of only four

people who have read *Midnight Sun*, which was an invaluable help to him, but Robert went further in his preparation for the film shoot. The shoot took six months, and locations were primarily small towns in the backwoods of Oregon. There would be a personal trainer to help keep him in shape, but when the *Evening Standard* talked to Robert a few months before he left for the shoot, they quizzed him about whether he'd be bored out in the unpopulated wilds, and asked what he was going to take with him to keep entertained. "I hope I'll have the courage not to take anything with me at all," he told them. "I want to be a bit monkish about it and focus completely on the work. I'll try to get up each morning at five thirty and go running." It's that kind of commitment that made Robert stand out to Catherine among the thousands of other guys who auditioned for Edward's role in the first place. "It's radical. They're living and breathing these characters," she told Andrew Sims of darkhorizons.com during his set visit.

Of course Edward has relationships with other characters besides Bella, and Robert wanted to understand those just as thoroughly as the romantic relationship. When Stephenie visited the set of the movie, he took full advantage of picking the endless source of backstory about these characters—her brain! He particularly wanted to know more about Edward's bond with the rest of the Cullen family. He told MTV, "The main thing I asked her is why Edward has accepted Carlisle as he has. He sometimes treats him as his father and sometimes as a sort of partner. I was just wondering why this 108-year-old guy would pretend to be a seventeen-year-old boy to someone who knows that he's not seventeen. And she said that Edward has judged Carlisle to be a good enough person to deserve him acting like his son—which I thought was very interesting. It's a very, very strange thing to do, if you have absolutely no relation to someone, and [to keep up the charade], just because they've stolen your soul against your will. Edward has found it within himself to forgive him to such an extent. . . . There aren't many scenes that show that, but I thought it was an interesting dynamic."

That's the kind of actor that Robert Pattinson is—one who goes to all lengths to understand his character as a full and rounded human (well, *inhuman*) being. Acting is much more than finding the perfectly timed delivery of lines or catching a costume in just the right light. For him, it's about adding layers of subtlety and understanding that are completely unspoken in the movie's dialogue, but live just beneath the surface of his character, adding to his performance in countless ways. Every gesture and moment and thought counts to Robert, and he'll do anything he can to make sure his performance is the best that he can possibly give.

Giving the part of Edward his all was more uncomfortable at some points than others. Sure, cuddling on a bed with Kristen or sitting beside her in biology lab was easy for Robert—far less torturous than the vampire Edward would have found those times being beside the girl he craved in every way possible. But Edward has an edge on Rob, too—he can leap and move unbelievably fast without having to be hooked up to wires. In an interview with G4.com, Robert admitted that, for as much as he understood why all the touchy-feely emotional parts of the story were so important, his wish would definitely be to get to do more "vampire stuff." Like any guy, he likes the fast pace, likes the action, and likes acting the hero.

Unlike the deadliest vamps in Stephenie Meyer's world, Edward is a "good" vampire, who doesn't attack crowds of people, and mostly tries to be as humanlike as possible. "It's cool when I get to do actual vampire stuff," Robert said to G4.com excitedly. Ironically, though, the real-life Robert is more like Bella than Edward. He told MTV that Kristen was the together one, and he was the klutz always messing everything up. And to G4.com he revealed, "I'm terrible at stunts. I've picked up so many injuries during this job. Nothing terrible, just sort of terminal groin chafing from harnesses. You always wear groin padding if you're a vampire." Ouch! Even though the action stunts sound and look cool, maybe Robert should be grateful he didn't have to do much more than he had to, after all. And maybe we'll just wipe the image of groin padding from our heads *right now*!

Rob and Rachelle Lefevre, who plays Victoria, one of the wild vampires, elaborated more about the vampire stunts in other interviews. They both say that wirework is much harder than it looks. To *Premiere* magazine, Robert said, "You would think it's kind of easy because you're essentially being pulled around, but it's very difficult to even maintain your center of gravity because you have to really fight against it as well as letting it do what it needs to do." Rachelle added, "Someone else is in control of your forward motion, which is a little disorienting." It sounds a lot like Edward's struggle to be around Bella, so even the discomfort of wirework probably led Robert to nuanced realizations about his portrayal of his character. "It's one of the hardest things I've ever done," Robert said. "I've done wirework in other stuff, but normally you're just getting hit and you just fall over and it doesn't really matter what happens because anyone can fall. But with the stunts in this, you have to look good and you have to look like you're doing it, so it's kind of tough." That's true—Robert had to look consistently perfect at all times as Edward, no matter how difficult the work. Perhaps he looked back to his days as Cedric underwater for the lessons of *that* experience to help him through this one.

Besides just because it's hard and sometimes inconvenient doesn't mean that the cast members disliked doing the stunt work. For actors as serious about their work as the *Twilight* cast is, any new challenge is something to make the most of—and totally conquer. Rachelle told MTV, "My favorite has got to be the wirework. They put you in a harness and put you on wires, and you're flying through the air. It's really amazing. We also do this thing called 'riding the magic carpet,' which makes you look like you're moving extremely fast. They make you walk at incredible speeds, on an incredibly fast-moving thing, so that the effect is like you're walking with no effort at thirty miles an hour." Sounds like watching themselves moving with inhuman grace and preternatural speed was just as much a thrill for Robert and his friends as it is for *Twilight* moviegoers everywhere.

Special effects weren't necessary only for fight scenes and the vampires' movements, however. There's also the sparkling skin to take into consideration. In Stephenie Meyer's vampire mythology, vampires are like stone, and they sparkle in the sunlight. How did the makeup and special-effects team create the dazzling Edward that Twilighters love? Before the movie was released, even Robert didn't know! "I haven't actually seen that yet," he told one interviewer. "It is CG [computer graphics], but I don't know what it's going to look like. That was one of the hardest things to do. We did like a thousand different ideas. We did this thing with flakes of salt and every single thing [they could think of]. I remember they painted one of the PAs [production assistants] blue, which was kind of a confused direction," he continued, laughing. After following those various directions, including about forty different makeup tests—some good, some not—and months of work for just that one scene, the filmmakers arrived at the right solution. Robert is already flawless, but as the brilliant-skinned Edward in the meadow, he made hearts beat faster than ever before. Ah, the magic of the silver screen!

Life as a Vampire

"I think what this story represents is some sort of unconditional love ... there's nothing that can get in the way of each other, even if his natural instinct is to eat humans."
—Rachelle Lefevre (Victoria)

In a presentation at the 2007 Brigham Young University Symposium on Books for Young Readers, several months before the official movie news was announced, but at the urging questions of fans, Stephenie Meyer talked about her dream of seeing *Twilight* as a movie. "If they get just one scene right—if they do just *one* scene well—that would be good enough for me. Even if the movie ends up being a Western or something!"

We can't quite picture Rob Pattinson in a Western—though, hey, who knows what's in his acting future?—but we're certainly glad that's *not* what happened to *Twilight*.

From the start, director Catherine Hardwicke set her ambitions higher than getting just *one* scene right. In an interview with the *Twilight* Lexicon, she explained why getting things right mattered so much to her, saying, "I love the book too, you know—I just want to make it come alive." But she had confidence in her work because of her love for it. As she told *Entertainment Weekly* online, "Luckily, I'm one of the fans, too and I loved it too, and that's a good starting point. So if I'm loving it, and I'm feeling like it's real, okay, then I'm halfway there, at least." But she knew that she had a real challenge ahead of herself, just the same. Turning a 544-page novel into a movie under two hours? Not exactly simple! But Catherine, who has directed many acclaimed films, knows her art of filmmaking well, and quickly realized that events and emotional developments that took pages and pages to develop in the book could actually sometimes be conveyed in a few words—or even a glance—on-screen. And the setting, which took Stephenie pages upon pages to write, doesn't need any description at all in the movie—it's simply present from the opening scenes, sweeping readers into the story.

Another challenge Catherine faced as a director was taking a story that had been narrated in the first person, by Bella, and turn it into a movie where we see everything happening in the world around and outside her. The cameras—and then the movie audience—will see far more than just what's in Bella's head, or what she sees. This was a challenge that delighted Catherine, though. As she eagerly chattered to aintitcoolnews.com, "Some stuff that's in Bella's head, I wanted to make it visual and take you out and feel the power of Edward and what he can do. When he says, 'You should be scared of me,' I want you to feel that, an adrenaline rush in your bones!"

And Stephenie Meyer feels that Catherine met that challenge head-on; she loves how moments like that work in the movie. As she told *Entertainment Weekly* online, "It was nice to get some of that really hardcore action worked in that she [Bella] couldn't have seen." Why was that great for a guy like Rob? Easy— more fight scenes!

One of the most important things that Catherine did as a director was help all of the actors understand their roles as characters first, and vampires second. Many of the actors have commented on how this led them to a power and energy that can't be missed on the screen. Rachelle Lefevre, who plays, as she calls it, "the female badass nomadic vampire," told teenhollywood.com, "In Stephenie's world, you have to find your character first and then go, 'Who was I before [I became a vampire], and how would I be, as a result of this virus that I got?' If you work just from starting with the vampire, it's all surface. It's not anything. . . . So we all worked really hard to figure out who we were, within the confines of that world, and then just added the vampire on top." It's coaching like this that surely helped Robert go deep into his understanding the character of Edward as a troubled and self-loathing quasi-monster.

Robert also understood that there needed to be more than one layer to his portrayal of Edward, or else Edward would be viewed as very good-looking, but ultimately very boring. So he dug deep into Edward's conflicted psyche to understand the tension which he lives with every day. And what he realized was very deep, indeed! As he told joblo.com during a set-visit interview, "I guess kind of the thing which I found interesting is that Edward is essentially the hero of this story but violently denies that he is the hero. Like at every point even when he does heroic things he still thinks that he's a complete—selfish—like the most ridiculously selfish evil creature around. He refuses to accept Bella's love for him but at the same time can't help but just kind of need it, which is kind of what the essential storyline is." The idea of playing such a conflicted character was part of what intrigued Robert about the role, because he added, "I liked it because there's not many stories which have a character who is in love with the thing you want to destroy the most, and you know, walking the incredibly fine line between choices like that." Whoa. Those are some deep, soulful thoughts from our vampire friend. But since vampires don't need sleep, they have more time to think about things like this than the rest of us, right?

So what else was important about the way Catherine Hardwicke trained her actors? Physicality, or the way her actors move on-screen, was incredibly important to her. As Cam Gigandet, who plays the role of James, the ultimate in purely evil vampires (and Bella's and Edward's archenemy), explained to premiere.com, "We actually watched numerous cat videos, like tigers and lions and all sorts of things, because they move with such a grace and speed and power and make it look so easy. Not that we're running around like cats, but there's that movement. It's very fluid, so we worked on that as much as we possibly could. And we even worked with a dance choreographer to get in touch with our bodies." Ashley Greene, who plays Alice Cullen, commented on this, too, saying, "The first two weeks I was in Oregon was strict training; there was no shooting. There was a lot of baseball, because there's a baseball scene. Then we did wire-work, and a lot of stuff to get us into the feeling of moving like a vampire. There were a couple of dance and movement classes." Likewise, Rachelle chimed in to MTV, with an added explanation of why that kind of work was basic but important—and the building blocks on which their characters were being created. "Catherine is very organic, and she really wants us to have it in our bodies about what it would be like to be a vampire. They have supernatural abilities beyond living forever. They have super-strength and speed and hearing and agility. So Catherine really wanted us to feel what that would be like. And so there's been a huge emphasis on having the vampires work together and rehearsing together to get this cohesiveness."

And, just as bonding was an important part of the process for Robert and Kristen, the actors playing the Cullen family had a bond to build, too. Even though she's outside the Cullen family circle, Rachelle understood this, telling MTV, "We've had cast dinners where we go out, just to bond—especially for the actors playing the Cullens. I think it's really important to them to be a family." Catherine added to that bond in small but important ways, too. For example, the Cullens each wear a version of a specially designed family crest—as a pendant, a ring, a bracelet—to remind them of the promises they have made to one another and of their status as "royal family" among vampires. As Catherine explained to joblo.com, "They don't go for traditional [vampires'] dark clothes. The Cullens wear these form-fitting clothes to draw attention to their beauty, and kind of colors like an arctic wolf. Like silvers, blues, grays, white and they kind of shimmer and they're sort of fabulous." And she paid equally close attention to every detail on the set, like the creation of the Cullens' hidden forest tree house, which sets a mood of mysterious timelessness for the entire movie.

But the one thing that even a meticulous director like Catherine Hardwicke couldn't control about her filmmaking? The weather! And that's not a surprise, because when Stephenie Meyer was writing *Twilight*, she did an Internet search to find the rainiest locale in the U.S. in which to set her story—in order to give the Cullens the most sunlight-free days possible. But she probably wasn't thinking then about the challenge it would create years down the line for moviemakers! The weather *was* a major challenge—maybe one of the biggest challenges of the entire moviemaking process. In her official blog about the movie filming, greetingsfromtwilight.com, Catherine recounts it all with as good a sense of humor as possible. "We survived snow, hail, sleet, torrential downpours, and blazing sun (when we didn't want it)—sometimes all in one day. SEVERE WEATHER is an understatement. The California actors weren't used to the Oregon winter—they had to wear wetsuits and double Smart-Socks to keep toasty. (How many places on your body can you put those chili pepper Heat Packs?) In one shooting day you could have rain, hail, snow, and SUNSHINE—not good for vampires! Talk about a filmmaker's challenge, trying to get all the shots in the same scene to match." Nearly every actor has talked in one interview or another about his or her less-than-fond memories of the cold, wet, damp of their days on set. And they're not exaggerating! In fact, an intern who visited the set recounts in her blog that "99 percent of the cast and crew agreed today was the worst day of filming they've ever been in."

In an interview with twilightlexicon.com, Katie, a movie double, or stand-in, for Kristen, answered a question about her favorite parts of making the movie: "The inside parts! Where it's not freezing and raining!" Poor Rob himself had a brutal weather-related experience of his own—so much time exposed to the elements led to a nasty case of bronchitis for him, mid-filming. Rob told teenhollywood.com that "Oregon has the strangest weather stuff that happens, especially in the spring, when we were shooting. It would be sunny, snowing, raining, and hailing, at exactly the same time. Though it could be raining, there'd be no clouds in the sky. It was like fake weather. Every two minutes, the weather would change." Rob's hometown of London is notoriously gray, rainy, and damp, so for him to go on at such lengths about Oregon's miserable weather? It must have been awful!

Still, everyone involved tried to stay in the best spirits possible, despite the frigid temperatures. At one point, visitors to the set recounted that when Catherine needed to get an important shot but the weather simply wasn't cooperating, she had all the actors and extras and stagehands get together to do a "storm dance," intended to sway the weather gods to grant the change needed to allow filming to go on. And the dance worked! Later that evening, the finally warm cast and crew were caught spontaneously cheering and rejoicing in the background of an MTV video interview with Michael Welch. Catherine had just announced that the necessary filming on the wicked-cold beach was finished and there would be no need to return. Yet, even with all the inconvenience, there's no doubt that the somber weather added to the atmosphere of the movie as a whole. Now that it's over, the stars—especially Rob—will surely spend so much time in the spotlight that the chilly moments on set will all seem worth it.

For teens living in the dreary-weathered Pacific Northwest, knowing that Robert Pattinson was just a few miles away for several months—and may well be back, if the sequels that everyone is hoping for get put into production—must have been a real thrill. While the small towns on the Washington coast featured in the books were visited by a few dozen devoted fans each month for the past few years, the filming changed things in a major way, even *before* the movie hit theaters. Some of the things were small touches— for example, the Miller Tree Inn, which town officials designated as representative of the Cullen home for their Forks tours, includes the Cullen name on the mailbox, and a sign near the door that includes a daily note signed by "Esme Cullen," explaining the reason that the Cullens aren't home. Some days, the sign tells visitors that the Cullens are out playing baseball. On others it reads, "Dr. Cullen is not in today. He and the family have gone hunting. In an emergency please call 911 or proceed to Forks Community Hospital." And if you stop by Forks Community Hospital, you'll see a parking spot with a sign marked DR. CULLEN: RESERVED PARKING ONLY.

Once they understood the attention, local businesses were quick to reach out to fans—creating lots of Forks- and *Twilight*-themed souvenirs. What's the most popular Forks souvenir of all? According to

Peninsula Daily News, it's a bumper sticker saying, FORKS BITES! Fans are hungry for more than just souveniors, though—*The Seattle Times* reports that Sully's, the local burger joint, sells close to one hundred "Bella Burgers" on a daily basis now, and the local Subway sandwich shop has jumped on board, too, creating a "*Twilight* Special" sandwich, complete with a bloody-looking marinara sauce. And Bella Italia, where Edward takes Bella for her first date, now includes mushroom ravioli on its menu, and has hosted visits from Stephenie Meyer, and the cast and crew, too. In 2007, the mayor of Forks declared September 13 (Bella's birthday) to be the town's official Stephenie Meyer Day, in honor of the books and the effect they'd had on the local area. The event is sure to get bigger each year; 2008's Stephenie Meyer Day hosted thousands of fans and two *Twilight*-themed bands, and an all-out celebration that drew visitors from all over the world. Perhaps an official Robert Pattinson Day won't be far behind, once the movie makes Forks an even more sought-after destination!

But the excitement in Oregon, where much of the filming took place, and neighboring Washington, where the story is set (and where some of the filming happened too), hasn't just been about businesses selling more T-shirts and sandwiches than usual. For some lucky residents, Bella and Edward's school is also *their* school. Although Catherine Hardwicke's team of location scouts had toured the actual Forks High in Washington in great detail, the decision was ultimately made to use two other schools, in neighboring Oregon, as the primary sites for filming school scenes. Forks High School got to represent in a small way, though. Several letter jackets belonging to actual Forks High School students were borrowed by the movie's costuming department and worn by actors during filming, but sadly, the jacket owners did not get to be extras themselves. And the Forks mascot *(Go Spartans!)* shows up on the gym floor, thanks to large stickers that did the convincing job of making an alternate gym look like it was the actual Forks High School.

So if the movie stars have *body* doubles, what schools played the, erm, *building doubles* for Forks High School? Madison High School, in Portland, Oregon (home of the Senators!), was the lucky location to be transformed into a fictional Forks High School on the inside, while Kalama Middle-High School in Washington *(Yay Chinooks!)* was used for exterior shots and a few other scenes. Imagine watching the movie knowing that Robert has sat in a classroom where you, too, spend your days. You certainly wouldn't be able to think of biology class in the same way!

Other movie-related facts have peppered the conversation of locals for months, as the whole Pacific Northwest got swept up in the excitement of a blockbuster movie being filmed in their own backyard. The actual logo for the town of Forks was reproduced for the sides of Police Chief Charlie Swan's car and uniform. And some lucky locals got to participate in the movie in a variety of ways. Eight La Push locals were cast as a particularly talented group of extras—surfers riding the waves in the background of the scene in which Jacob tells Bella about the Quileute legends. And other area locals were cast as extras for school scenes, and in other jobs, such as being body doubles for Robert, Bella, and Jacob. According to Lana Veenker, one of the casting directors for *Twilight*, who answered questions for Twilighters on her blog and on the *Twilight* Lexicon site, the casting crew had their eyes on several of the young hopefuls who answered the local casting call for Jacob Black. Even though they ultimately decided to cast the more experienced Taylor Lautner in the role, Catherine and her casting directors may well reconnect with some of the locals who auditioned, should the next few movies get made, since there will be a need for more wolfpack boys.

So what does Rob think of all the excitement he caused across two states? Well, it seems he was a real gentleman of an actor while in town. Fan sites across the Internet show him kindly posing with enthusiastic fans who came to the filming sites, even though all those many encounters probably added up to a lot *more* time for him to be out in the damp and frigid weather he hated. A *Twilight* Mom posted on twilightinternational.com about Rob's kindness during her son's visit to the set, "He said Rob was very friendly and very gracious and was concerned that Sean and another girl had been seen standing in the rain and cold all day." And clearly Rob has a sense of humor about all the attention, too. One blogger wrote of the encounter she and her two friends had upon being seated *right next to* Rob and Jackson Rathbone, who plays Jasper, at a local restaurant in Kalama. The trio didn't get up the courage to ask for a photo with him, but they did ask him to take a picture of the three of them together. Robert obliged quite willingly, and told them, "Say you love me!" as he shot the photo. *Swoon.* If only every Rob-lover could have such a chance!

R̄ob the Heartthrob!

"I think the most challenging thing for me on set was to keep myself from falling deep into the spell of Robert Pattinson's dark, yellowish, mystical eyes. ::sigh::" —*Michael Welch*

Heartthrob. Hunkola. Hottie. Heart-meltingly handsome. Sizzling. Smokin'! Juicy man candy. Sugarlips. Stud Muffin. Hott! *Swoon.*

Yes, once you start thinking about Robert Pattinson, it's hard to stop. Add the fact that Rob Pattinson *is* Edward Cullen, and it's no wonder that he's what many of us consider the ultimate pinnacle of boyfriend potential. (Sorry, Team Jacob, but it's just a total fact.) Even the creator of vampiric perfection herself agrees!

After a visit to the movie set, Stephenie Meyer reported back to her fans, gushing with admiration for Kristen and Rob, and warning, "You might want to bring a paper bag to the movie, because the on-screen chemistry may cause hyperventilation."

But all the adoration and attention are no surprise for those who have been following Robert's rise since his breakthrough as Cedric Diggory in *Harry Potter and the Goblet of Fire*. In a 2005 article titled, "Almost Famous," *The Times* [London] cast their vote for RPattz, as some fans have dubbed him, early on, stating, "This fresh-faced, photogenic 18-year-old so oozes charm and likeability that casting directors are predicting a big future." And later that year, *Times* Online voted him "British Star of Tomorrow." In recent months, movie fans and industry watchers alike have been comparing Rob's rapidly building stardom and seemingly endless amounts of potential to the similar way Leonardo DiCaprio and Jude Law catapulted onto movie-star A-lists. Already the online film journal themovie-fanatic.com has named him "The Hottest Young Actor" of the year.

Even so, the attention has come as a bit of a shock to Rob himself. The twenty-two-year-old tends to laugh when he's nervous, and nearly every time he's asked about the increasing amounts of fandom focused on him, he stammers, blushes, stalls by combing his fingers through his trademark messy hair, and punctuates his sentences with nervous chuckles. Since this has made for countless video interviews and photos filled with Rob's rakishly charming smile, though, it's just one more reason we think he's lovable. You'd expect someone as suave and mellow as Rob to take all the attention in stride, but he's actually been overwhelmed to the point of (adorable) shyness by the constant spotlight. He understands it all, he thinks—well, sort of—and maybe as much as any guy can. "It's the character that they like. . . . It's just really strange how Edward has such a connection with girls." But as he told teenhollywood.com, "I still can't really come to terms with it. As soon as one person recognized me, I started freaking out. Wherever I go, I freak out. Even when people come up, they're always really nice . . . but, for some reason, I'm just a good freaker-outer. I just freak out, all the time."

The truth is, even though he's a rapidly up-and-coming actor with literally millions of fans, Robert Pattinson is really just a humble guy from London who isn't quite sure what all the fuss is about when it comes to himself. Oliver Irving, the director of *How to Be*, a movie Rob made just before embarking on the filming of *Twilight*, put it this way in an interview with themovie-fanatic.com, "It was funny because he told us he had a part in a *Harry Potter*, but as you can imagine, many actors in England have had tiny parts in those films. Plus he really underplayed it so I didn't think much of it at the time. It wasn't until we had cast him [that] I watched the *Harry Potter* film he was in and realized he was a major part." And back in those same *Harry Potter* days, Rob told BBC's News

Round program, "If I was Katie [Leung], I would definitely go out with Daniel [Radcliffe] because he's rich and famous, and I'm not, really." Well, times have changed, and even Robert knows that he can't really claim to be "not famous" anymore. But even with all the hype surrounding *Twilight*, he's kept a wry sense of humor about all the focus on his looks. As he laughingly told teenhollywood.com, "When you read the description of Edward, it says he's so beautiful, it hurts to look at him. It's difficult to act that, so I wouldn't really know how to go about doing it. I hope there's been a lot of postproduction airbrushing!" How charming that a looker like Rob thinks he needs even a little airbrushing.

Robert understands the attraction to vampires, at least. He explained to teenhollywood.com that he's not immune to the sort of visceral reaction that makes the idea of a vampire scream, "HOTT!!!" Of course, he put it slightly more coherently, explaining, "There is something really sexy about, like, the whole vampire image is something sucking your neck." We certainly agree!

Speaking of sexy moments, various interviewers have asked Kristen the question we all want to know: What's it like kissing the hotness that is Rob/Edward? But Robert's happy to answer that question himself. As he explains to MTV, "Everything starts off very kiddie, very tame. It's supposed to be very sweet. Then it turns into, like, hell. Like all kisses do. Basically whenever we kiss, I just try to kill her all the time." That's a risk a lot of his fans would be willing to take, though, especially when Robert offers juicy tidbits like he did in an interview with premiere .com. When that interviewer asked, "How did you approach the kissing scenes? Tongue or no tongue?" Robert answered boldly and without missing a beat, "I always try to slip a bit of tongue in!"

So when he's not busy making out with or trying to kill Bella, who is the lucky gal on the other side of Robert's kisses? When asked by a rather cheeky reporter at the *Goblet of Fire* premiere, "Are you single?" Robert's reply spoke volumes, "Um, ack, it's sort of difficult," he stammered, with lots of blushing and a bit of hesitation. Clearly there was *someone* in his life at that moment, even if the persistent watchers on *Harry Potter* fan sites were never able to confirm Robert's reported romances. Sigh. Who wouldn't love even a semiofficial "It's Complicated" status with Robert?

He did respond via an MTV interview to the slew of *Twilight* fans who have proclaimed their undying love and desire to marry him, though, with a bit of a tongue-in-cheek answer. "It depends on what you look like. No, not really. Well . . ." He laughed, but continued, "It's depending on how old you are and on a lot of other things." And he warned his potential suitors, "I don't like children, though; not at all," a fact confirmed by several snapshots that have been posted to fan forums, where Robert is posed next to a smiling mother and baby, but making a face as if he were going to eat the baby! Robert rounded out his wish list for desirable qualities in a girlfriend with a request that makes perfect sense for an actor. "And you'd have to clap after every take on every job I do for . . . the rest of my life." Think you fit the bill? Well, get in line, ladies!

Rob's appreciation for pretty girls, fashion, and acting are all tied up together, it seems, just as much of the fan love for him comes from a combined adoration for his pretty face and his many artistic abilities as musician, model, and actor. Even at age fifteen, he knew that snazzy accessories like his favorite red suede shoes got him "loads of attention," and no one who's gotten even a glimpse at the spreads from his modeling days can deny that this is a guy who wears a fine suit *exceedingly* well. When asked in a British interview about the "flash clothes" (heart that British slang!) he wore during the Yule Ball scene at the Harry Potter movie, Robert was delighted to talk about his customized wizard tuxedo, saying, "I feel like Dracula! It's nice." Hmm, perhaps Robert has had a penchant for vampires all along?

But as the photos we've seen and drooled over clearly portray, he's equally at home being in jeans and T-shirts as he is in designer fashion. In fact, getting dressed up for movie premieres sometimes makes him feel "like a girl," as he's laughingly told reporters on the red carpet at movie premieres. So it might not be *too* much of a stretch to suggest that perhaps what he likes best about fashion is, well, the models. He's quipped to *Teen People*, "Looking for supermodels takes up my time," and his jest may not be so very far from the truth! Though they're not a couple these days, he's been linked romantically with Nina Schubert, a German model, who works for the high-end fashion agency Elite Models. Since Robert's done fashion and modeling work as well, theirs was an obvious match, but with both of them having such demanding schedules, it's not hard to understand why he's stopped being seen with her in public. After all, a long-distance, cross-continent relationship would be hard for anyone to maintain!

But it's not just the supermodel type that catches his eye, or so we suspect. Currently the state of Rob's love life has been a bit of a mystery, and we expect it's a mystery that Robert's cultivated on purpose. When quizzed by an interviewer on the *Twilight* set whether there are any "hidden deep dark secrets" about his own personal life that he tries to "keep under wraps," Rob carefully dodged that potentially revealing question by deflecting it into another area altogether, stating that he "spends his life" trying to hide the fact that he can sometimes be a complete jerk. Not that we believe that for a split second! But he went on to explain a bit of why he tries to keep his most personal facts out of the tabloids, saying, "If you tell everybody all your secrets and all your phobias and all the scars in your closet and go around telling them all that, then they think you've got even better stuff [still hidden]." That's not a bad point—clearly Rob understands that a life lived fully in the spotlight can become overwhelming for even the most balanced of stars. Or, maybe it just means that Robert hasn't dated the right kind of girls yet, since he laughingly told one video interviewer on the set of *Twilight*, "Most girls I do fall for end up being vampires."

But, even though his fans care about Rob and respect his privacy, it doesn't stop them from being intrigued, and from speculating about his future—including his romantic future—just the same! Of course he's been linked with his costars, and fans of *Harry Potter* and *Twilight* alike would love nothing more than to see him re-create his on-screen romance with Katie Leung or Kristen Stewart in real life. But even though neither of those relationships seems to have blossomed into full romance, there's a lot that Rob-watchers can piece together about the kind of girl who *would* be his dream girl. Studying Rob's easy-going friendships with the ladies reveals a lot.

Robert spends a lot of time out with his friends,

and so has naturally been linked with all of his girl friends as supposed *girlfriends* at various times. He's been photographed laughing and partying with actress Camilla Belle, but the fact that people think they're dating surely makes him laugh, because she's actually the girlfriend of his "best mate," Tom Sturridge. And although he and Katie Leung don't see each other on a regular basis anymore, he's kept in close contact with his former costar. He definitely values long-term loyalty like the friendship that has deepened between them over the years since they filmed *Goblet of Fire* together. Plus he's said over and over in interviews that Kristen Stewart is one of the main reasons he wanted the part of Edward, so it's clear that girls who are full of passion and at the top of their game impress him. That's no surprise, really. Robert has worked hard to become the best actor he can be, so a similar devotion to ambition is understandably something he's looking for in a potential girlfriend. He's told interviewers that he loves girls who will "pick fights with me" (which seems clear from the playful teasing and banter he's engaged in with Kristen during joint interviews) and can't stand girls who "are aloof."

So, what does all the mystery about Rob's love life add up to? Perhaps it's the fact that right now, he's most focused on his career. Though the world is full of hopeful young actors, there are few who have skyrocketed to fame the way that Robert has, and he knows he should take advantage of all the opportuni ties awaiting him. Maybe it means that he knows that a career like his makes it all too hard to remain in the same place for long enough to maintain the kind of strong relationship he wants. Being able to truly treat a girlfriend right is really important to him, and for the last three years, he's lived on three continents—in Europe, where his family and deepest roots are in England; in Africa, where he spent time filming in South Africa; and now in North America, where he's been introduced to U.S. locales like soggy Oregon and busy LA. Maybe he's waiting to decide whether his music wins out over his acting—and wants to know himself better before he goes looking for a soulmate. Or, perhaps, not unlike the Edward of our dreams, Robert is simply still holding out for the perfect girl . . . though certainly we hope Rob won't have to spend 108 years waiting for his Bella!

What's Next for Rob . . .
And for *Twilight*?

"I did lean over to Rob today in the middle of the screaming and say, 'I apologize for what I've done to your life.'" —*Stephenie Meyer*

August 2, 2008, was a day that millions of fans had long awaited, marking it with countdown widgets on their blogs, Facebook pages, and MySpace accounts. Why? Because it was the release day (or night, actually—books couldn't be sold until 12:01 a.m. that Friday night) for *Breaking Dawn,* the fourth and final book in the Twilight Saga, heralded with midnight proms, major rock concerts, and thousands of anxious and excited readers lined up to find out the long-awaited ending to Edward and Bella's story. Will moviegoers have the same opportunity? Will Robert Pattinson and Kristen Stewart steam up the silver screen as Edward and Bella in three more movies? *Twilight* author Stephenie Meyer revealed to MTV that she'd love for that to happen—but she thinks that *Breaking Dawn* would have to be split into two movies. (And she knows just where *she* would do it, but wouldn't say!) So in Stephenie's dream world, we could have a total of five movies about Edward and Bella.

That might be *everyone's* dream world, in fact, because who wouldn't want that much more Robert? It would definitely keep the vampire hottie in the public eye for quite some time to come! "There's so many things that would be interesting to see," Stephenie continued in the MTV interview. "One of my favorite scenes of the whole series is in the tent in *Eclipse*, the fire-and-ice chapter. Oh, I do want to see that! There's a lot of things, visually, that are so much cooler than you can do in a book." Kristen Stewart and Robert both have their own dream scenes from the following books, too. Kristen told MTV, "The second book opens pretty cool. It opens with a birthday party, and I cut my finger, and the whole Cullen family goes into a frenzy. And then it's like, 'OK, we need to figure out how to make this work, because this isn't.' I think that's going to be a cool visual." Robert added, "I want to do the killing myself scene in Italy. That'll be fun. I think that'll be quite exciting." Good thing faithful fans know that Edward doesn't *really* kill himself, though, or there might be a public outcry from RPattz fans worldwide.

How close to a reality are future *Twilight* films? Well, the CEO of Summit Entertainment, Rob Friedman, teased the website shocktillyoudrop.com with, "We're talking about it." That may be cryptic enough to be infuriating, but Summit's devotion is already a cold, hard, vampire fact. The production company has optioned both *New Moon* and *Eclipse*, and is interested in optioning *Breaking Dawn*. "Optioning" the movie adaptation rights of a novel means that the production company has paid for the *option* of making that adaptation. Because the company hasn't committed to producing the movie, most options are for a set amount of time, and then they expire. When that happens, the option can either be renewed, or another company can option the movie rights.

Of course, since *Twilight* is poised to be the biggest teen movie of the season, it's very likely that Summit will green-light (go ahead with) the movie adaptation of *New Moon* with barely a second thought. One *Twilight* producer, Wyck Godfrey, takes that a step further. "The goal is, we've got the [sequel] script ready to go and come December we want to shoot it for about the same time—for the weather and stuff, we don't want to be in the heart of the winter. Obviously, you know the next book and know we can go out into the sun a little bit more. Hopefully, we'll have it ready to go and ready to start prepping for the beginning of next year." While it's still all rumor and conjecture, and nothing has been confirmed, it all sounds only positive. One thing is certain—millions of fans' fingers are crossed, and waiting for the news they're hoping to hear.

There's one more *Twilight*-related project in the misty future: *Midnight Sun*, the *Twilight* story told from Edward's point of view. *Twilight* is told entirely from inside Bella's head, but *Midnight Sun* reveals what the very same scenes look like from inside Edward's. The first chapter is posted on Stephenie's website, and of course Robert got to see about ten chapters more of the unfinished manuscript. Though showing her unfinished manuscript had to have been a very scary, vulnerable decision for Stephenie, it's also one that made perfect sense to her. As she told *Entertainment Weekly*, "I wanted [Robert and Catherine Hardwicke] to have every single thing that could help them make it feel right." Stephenie has gone on to say, "If I'd realized how much more fun it is to tell the story from a vampire point of view, I'd have started there." She has no publication schedule for *Midnight Sun*, since she hasn't sold it to her publisher yet. "It's for me still," she told *Entertainment Weekly.* "I'll probably sell it when I'm done, for one reason: I want to have it bound up on my shelf with the others. Or maybe I'll just publish it on my website."

Until we know future *Twilight* movie plans, though, how will we possibly get our Robert fix? Robert Pattinson is not the kind of guy to sit idly around, so there will be plenty of ways to both see and hear him in the coming year. For one, *Twilight*'s Edward isn't Rob's only starring role this fall. He also has two—yes! two!—independent films releasing this fall. After the eleven-month shoot playing Cedric in *Harry Potter and the Goblet of Fire,* Robert was yearning for a less-expansive project. "My instinct at the end was just to sort of collapse. What I aim[ed] to do next is a really short shoot. A six-week thing where I can get my brain around the whole thing. A play or something," he said in one interview. That instinct led him to two indie flicks.

How to Be is about a young, frustrated musician named Arthur. It's a black comedy: Arthur's girlfriend has dumped him, and he has no other choice but to move back in with his parents after having gone away to school. No one is thrilled about that arrangement, obviously, and Arthur and his friend discover a self-help guru who they think can help them through it. Oliver Irving, director of *How to Be*, had a lot to say about Robert's role as Arthur: "It's about friendship, about music, trying to rise above mediocrity, but then it's about self-help. I knew people that were kind of leaving university, trying to get on with their lives, and trying to figure out what they were doing, and I also knew other people, older people, who were very into self-help. I was kind of drawing together lots of anecdotes. And that's one of the reasons why Robert Pattinson's Art[thur] works so well. He came at it from just trying to understand what it was about, he was playing a version of himself." It's a funny, painful, rich, and oddball film, and a fascinating switch to a quieter role, compared to the huge blockbusters Rob had been doing.

The team behind *How to Be* had been searching for their lead actor for more than a year, but as soon as they found Robert, they knew they had their guy. Oliver Irving told *The Movie Fanatic*, "I pretty much instantly knew he would be right. I think he forgot his lines and just started improvising which is exactly what I wanted—someone who could just become the character and leave behind the kind of 'techniques' trained in at drama schools." Irving feels strongly that anyone who watches *How to Be* will be treated to Robert's finest and most truthful performance to date. "As I say he seemed to fall into the part very easily and was up for exploring parts of his own persona and how his character would interact with the other," Irving said. "Rob definitely comes alive when the cameras roll though. His performances were always heightened by pressure—he would often in rehearsals say—okay it's not right now, but I know what is needed and I'll get it on the day. This took an awful lot of faith in him but he was pretty much true to his word."

The other film is called *Little Ashes*, an APT Films project about Spanish writers, artists, and filmmakers in the 1920s, in which Robert plays the renowned avant-garde artist Salvador Dali. Yes, the Salvador Dali whose great work "The Persistence of Memory" features liquid-looking clocks and graces art teachers' walls and dorm rooms around the world. *Little Ashes* may stray even further from Robert's previous work experience. The producers have called it both "racy" and "sexy"—but not in the way Twilighters might expect. The film depicts the gay love affair between Dali and Federico García Lorca, a Spanish dramatist and poet. "I think some people might be a bit surprised," Robert told the *Evening Standard*, prior to filming *Twilight*. "But I didn't want to get stuck in pretty, public school roles, or I knew I'd end up as some sort of caricature. Playing Dali has been a complete turning point for me. It's the first part I've had that has required really serious thought. I became completely obsessed with Dali during the filming, and I read every biography I could get a hold of. He was the most bizarre, complex man, but in the end I felt I could relate to him. He was basically incredibly shy." Robert's unafraid to stretch his acting chops, and this turning point will undoubtedly lead him to more challenging and interesting roles. Perhaps he was even thinking of his idol, Jack Nicholson, who also chose a wide variety of roles in which to showcase different sides of himself and to expand his own perception of his limits.

Robert clearly has the ambition to continue pushing his boundaries, and anything he does is bound to be spectacular. Yet, he also told the *Evening Standard* that he didn't necessarily want to be hugely famous. "I can't see any advantage to it, because I'm happy with the life I have now. I've got the same two friends I've had since I was twelve, and I can't see that changing," he says. He disclosed that he hates clothes shopping, doesn't have a car, and lives with a good friend in an apartment in London's Soho neighborhood. Most intriguingly, he revealed that he didn't currently have a girlfriend! With such a busy, globe-trotting life, it must be hard to keep a relationship going, but no doubt he'd try very hard for the right girl. Asked if he wanted to "raise hell" in the Hollywood scene, like so many other prominent young actors, Rob was dismissive. "I believe it's rather hard to raise hell in Hollywood now. If you have a second glass of wine, people think you're an alcoholic." His sensible attitude and his ambition prove that Robert's the well-rounded hottie that Twilighters had been waiting for.

Speaking of that ambition, not only did he reveal the juicy details of his personal life to the *Evening Standard*; he also mentioned some of his loftier career goals. Remember how Robert wasn't the best student while he was in school? Getting expelled when he was twelve, with his teachers claiming he didn't try very hard to get good grades? Well, he wishes he'd been a bit better about all that now. "I wasn't at all focused on school, and I didn't achieve much," he said. "But I've got a sense of urgency now. I feel I can't let any more time waste away." Starring in two massively popular movies, as well as having the courage to take on challenging roles in smaller films, isn't exactly being a couch potato, but Robert wants to do even more. He still remembers that favorite English teacher—who forced him to write rather than simply answer questions—and he wants to do right by that influence. His ten-year plan includes having his own production company and writing his own film. He's already begun one script, which is based on his teenage diaries. That project is with an American agent, so we may get to see Robert as a writer and star sooner rather than later.

And there's always his music. As he told MTV, it's difficult to maintain both his acting and his music, so he's thinking that he "might do it properly after the movie." He might go to Nashville. He's been "trying to write an album for years and years." Maybe this will be the time—if he can get away from his adoring public long enough to seclude himself in a studio. Not likely, Rob!

Even if Rob does briefly leave the Hollywood spotlight to chase his rock star dreams, luckily, his fans do have some other options to get their hottie fix. Between *Harry Potter and the Goblet of Fire* and *Twilight*, Robert performed in a short film called *The Summer House* and in two productions for British television. *Haunted Airman* is a chilling suspense tale based on the novel *The Haunting of Toby Jugg* by Dennis Wheatley. Flight Lieutenant Jugg was wounded in action and confined to a wheelchair. When he goes to a secluded mansion to recover, he's haunted by nightmares and visions, and doesn't know whom he can trust. *The Bad Mother's Handbook* is also an adaptation of a novel. This seems to be Robert Pattinson's specialty. He simply has that classic and true quality just right for embodying literary heroes.

In *The Bad Mother's Handbook*, Robert plays an intellectual boy named Daniel, who becomes the new best friend of a pregnant girl named Charlotte. The story is Charlotte's, and her mother's, and grandmother's—an intergenerational tale based on the novel by Kate Long. Such an estrogen-filled film must have been a change from the action-packed experience of *Goblet of Fire*, as was playing the role of a nerd instead of a heartthrob, but what an eye-opening time for Robert, where he could gain insights into the female mind!

But boys will be boys. One of the other future film options spinning around in Robert's head comes back around to action movies. "I always liked Gambit from *X-Men*," he told MTV. "Gambit would be cool. Has he ever been in an *X-Men* movie?" The interviewer responded, "He hasn't, but supposedly he's going to be in the *Wolverine* spin-off film." Good news for Robert, isn't it? He thought so: "I might have to get my foot in that door." You know, that might not be all bad! After all, most girls will have to drag their boyfriends to see *Twilight*, but *X-Men*? That's a little different! And guys everywhere would be thrilled—if a little perplexed—when their girlfriends demand to be taken to see the *Wolverine* movie.

Whatever comes next for Robert, whether it's more Edward (fingers crossed hard!), his music, or a role in a movie that we haven't even heard of or imagined yet, it's clear that he's just getting started. His devotion to his role as Edward has secured him a place in many hearts around the world, and so has his cheeky grin, messy hair, and all-around godlike appeal. So someday when he's an established major star who can't be missed, Twilighters will be proud to say, "We've loved him since the beginning!"

Bite-size Facts About Robert Pattinson

Everything you need to know about Rob in one bite!

Birthday: May 13, 1986

Height: 6'1"

Hometown: London, England

Zodiac sign: Taurus, the Bull (which means Rob is resourceful, loyal, sensual, musical, and artistic!)

Family: Mom, Clare; Dad, Richard; Two older sisters, Victoria and Lizzy

Nicknames: Rob, Patty (what his friends call him), RPattz (what fans call him—though *he* thinks it sounds "like an antacid pill"), Spunk Ransom (long story!)

Trademark feature: wildly messy hair

Hobbies: playing cards, darts, making music, listening to music, hanging with his mates, keeping journals

Shoe size: 10

If he weren't an actor, Rob would be: a pianist (or Jack Nicholson)

On-screen death scenes: One . . . so far!

Guilty pleasure: watching *American Idol*

Not a fan of: regimented exercise, shopping for clothes, rainy weather in Oregon, his name

Guaranteed to make him blush: 6,000 screaming fans

Rob's Favorites!

Actors: Jack Nicholson, Michael Gambon, Warwick Davis, Al Pacino

Restaurant: In-N-Out Burger

Superheroes: Spider-Man and *X-Men*'s Gambit

Teacher: His English teacher

Cartoons: *Sharkey & George* and *Hammertime*

Movie vampires: Max Schreck's *Nosferatu*; Gary Oldman's *Dracula*

Favorite thing about filming *Twilight*: Kristen Stewart; getting to do "vampire stuff"

Least favorite thing about filming *Twilight*: the weather!

Starring . . . Robert Pattinson
A Filmography

Need more Robert?

Start here.

Ring of the Nibelungs (2004) . . . . . Giselher

Vanity Fair (2004) . . . . . Rawdy Crowley

Harry Potter and the Goblet of Fire (2005) . . . . . Cedric Diggory

The Haunted Airman (2006) . . . . . Toby Jugg

The Bad Mother's Handbook (2007) . . . . . Daniel Gage

The Summer House (2008) . . . . . Richard

How to Be (2008) . . . . . Arthur

Twilight (2008) . . . . . Edward Cullen

Little Ashes (2009) . . . . . Salvador Dali

Twenty Places to Get Your RPattz Fix!

Twilight Sites

www.bellaandedward.com

www.hisgoldeneyes.com

www.twilightlexicon.com

www.twilightmoms.com

www.twilighters.org

Robert Pattinson Fan Sites

www.robert-pattinson.co.uk

www.robertpattinson.org

http://robert-pattinson.net/

http://robert-pattinson.info/

http://robertpattinsononline.com/

http://robpattinson.blogspot.com/

Official Sites

www.thetwilightsaga.com

www.twilightthemovie.com

www.stepheniemeyer.com

YouTube Channels

www.youtube.com/user/KristenWorld

www.youtube.com/user/teampattinson

www.youtube.com/user/skelletonkey

www.youtube.com/user/twilightvinculum

www.youtube.com/user/OfficialTwilightFilm

Good Old-Fashioned Fan Mail

Love letters and fan mail for Rob may be sent to:

Robert Pattinson

c/o Endeavor Agency

Stephanie Ritz

9601 Wilshire Blvd. Floor 3

Beverly Hills, CA 90210

USA